Finding the Lost Dalton

Your book is a fun read. A must for folks who hunger for colorful stories of the "real" Wild West.

—*Larry Foley*
Executive Producer of *Indians, Outlaws, Marshal's and the Hanging Judge* and Professor of Communication at the University of Arkansas

Finding the Lost Dalton is an important book documenting the location, circumstance, and murder of Deputy U.S. Marshal Frank Dalton. Dalton was one of the brave federal lawmen of the Fort Smith, Arkansas, federal court that worked for federal judge Isaac C. Parker. Dalton had brothers who worked with him as posse and after his death became legendary outlaws. Well researched by Trisler, this book will add to the knowledge of Frank Dalton's career and last days as a federal lawman in the Indian Territory. It is an important addition to the books on deputy U.S. marshals on the western frontier.

—*Art T. Burton*
Author of *Black, Red, and Deadly* and *Black Gun, Silver Star*

Mr. Trisler has taken us on an adventure into the process of uncovering history. Mr. Trisler in his own delightful way is dusting off and bringing new light to areas of scholarly research of the westward expansion.

—*Daniel Cockrell*
Executive Director, Old State House Museum, Division of Arkansas Heritage

Finding the Lost Dalton

Harold Trisler

Red Engine Press
Fort Smith, Arkansas

Copyright © 2023 Harold Trisler

ALL RIGHTS RESERVED. No part of this book may be reproduced or transmitted in any form or by any means, electronic or mechanical, including photocopying, recording, or by any information storage and retrieval system (except by a reviewer or commentator who may quote brief passages in a printed or on-line review) without permission of the publisher.

Contributor & Editor: David Higginbotham

Cover Art by Brett Short
Cover Design by Joyce Faulkner

Library of Congress Control Number: 2023941287
ISBN: 979-8-9879576-5-3 (softcover)

Foreword

For thirty years the author has been a strong advocate for the preservation and the public's education of the history of Arkansas and Oklahoma around Fort Smith. He and his family have put in countless hours on the grounds of the historic site presenting living history demonstrations on the U.S. Court proceedings, the Marshal Service as well as the outlaws and their victims; and he can portray a fur trapper or a soldier in the long military era represented in the park with equal aplomb. And over those thirty years he has always been a stickler for authenticity in his presentation and accuracy in the history he was portraying and explaining for the public.

In Western history, the Dalton outlaw family has always generated interest, and this is showcased in both print and on the movie screen, all with a wide range of historical accuracy. But Frank Dalton the lawman has always been the outlier in these efforts. It has often been thought that if he had not been murdered the other brothers might have never gone outlaw, at least to the degree they did. Frank deserves more attention than he has generated in the past and the author has started with the basic mystery, just where did he die. It shouldn't be that hard to figure out—it was only four miles from Fort Smith. But Harold's extended search showed just how hard it was. He has pretty well solved that part of the mystery, a major effort after almost 150 years and the changes that have occurred in the area. He also expands on the local history of the area right across from the Fort in the old Indian Territory, which should also be very much appreciated.

—Bill Black
Former Superintendent of the Fort Smith National Historic Site

Prologue

Fort Smith in the 1880s provides a snapshot of a changing America. While the state of Arkansas has roots in the South, Fort Smith has always embodied the spirit of westward expansion. As the 19th century waned, America choked the frontier in from all sides, and relations with Native Americans at the end of the Trail of Tears look nothing like the dime-store novels being penned by the journalists in Boston and New York who've never set foot outside of a city.

Life on the edge of the frontier was complicated. With civilization came an attempt at civilized justice. But Fort Smith, which earned the nickname "Hell on the Border," wasn't always civilized. The town, immortalized in *True Grit*, operated in two worlds.

Table of Contents

Foreword iii

Prologue iv

November 27, 1887 1

The Search 3

The Dark Year of 1887 17

A Brief Chronology of the Arkansas River 27

Indian Territory Deputies 33

The Courtroom 39

Notes from May 23, 2022 43

Analysis of the Shooting 46

The Event 52

Notes for the Chapter on Cole 56

Moffett -Exile across the River 67

After the Dalton Killing 72

Notes on why this matters today 80

In the middle of the night again – November 26, 2022 82

Appendix 84

About the Author 107

About the Contributor & Editor 109

Acknowledgements 110

November 27, 1887

Our story begins on a Sunday morning in late November in the Indian Territories. Two Deputy U.S. Marshals have caught wind of a fugitive close to home. Deputy James R. Cole and Deputy Frank Dalton both have warrants for Dave Smith, a man wanted for larceny and introduction of liquor into the Indian Nations, and word has spread that Smith is camped out just across the Arkansas River from Fort Smith, seat of the Western District Federal Court.

Smith, their sources say, isn't hiding. He is in a logging camp known locally as Payne's Clearing. The trip would be easy. The deputies could ride out and back in the same day.

Though Cole and Dalton had both begun their pursuits independently, they decided to ride to Payne's Clearing together.

There are seven adults in the camp this Sunday, and three children. This, though, isn't immediately apparent to the two lawmen riding into sight of the camp. At this time of the morning, no one is cutting timber or milling lumber. The clearing is quiet.

There is activity. A young woman sees the men riding in and steps back inside a large canvas tent.

Cole and Dalton dismount and split up. Cole approaches the tent from the north side. Deputy Dalton approached from the south.

Dalton reaches the tent first. He splits the tent flaps with the barrel of his Winchester and pushes inside.

The woman grabs the muzzle of the rifle and shoves it up. Dave Smith, the man the deputies have come for, is there, behind her. He fires at Deputy Dalton, hitting him once in the chest.

As Dalton falls backwards from the tent, Smith barrels over the wounded man and makes a break for the cover of the edge of the clearing.

Deputy Cole, though, has a clear shot. He steps out from behind the tent, levels his Winchester, and shoots Smith in the back. Smith falls on the spot.

Two others now run from the tent–a man and a woman. They both run to Smith. Deputy Cole shoots the woman as she bent over Smith's body. Then he shoots the man.

As this second round of gunfire erupts, others in the tent, run from the north end of the tent, away from the gun fight, and escape into the woods.

A fifth shot rings out from inside the tent, striking Cole. The wound, though, is superficial. The shot grazes his chest. Deputy Cole stumbles and trips over a tent stake, and falls. Having lost the advantage, Cole bolts for cover.

His path takes him past Dalton, who lies on the ground outside the tent. "Are you killed?" Cole yells to Dalton.

There is no reply.

As Cole reaches the cover of the trees at the edge of the clearing, he turns back to the camp. There is movement in the tent, so Cole shoots blindly into the canvas. He looks for movement from Dalton, but there is none.

More shots ring out from the tent, so Cole retreats. He rides for Fort Smith and reinforcements.

The last of the men inside the tent, the one who had almost taken down Cole, steps out with a rifle in his hand.

Dave Smith is dead. Two others are wounded. The sound of Cole racing back to Fort Smith has vanished.

Deputy Dalton, on his back, is still alive. "Don't kill me" he begs.

The man shoots Dalton in the face. Twice.

The Search

This is a Mystery...

I knew none of this story when I first noticed the Deputy's name on a cardboard marker outside of the most storied courtroom of the American west.

The humble tribute was only one of some fifty small placards placed to commemorate the Deputy Marshals killed in the line of duty during the Judge Parker court era, which lasted about two decades—1875 to 1895. Fort Smith, Arkansas is our hometown. Even though I had been to the historic site many times as a volunteer, I was struck by how little I knew of these men.

One name reached out to me with a story that seemed out of place—Frank Dalton.

The Daltons I knew were outlaws. The Dalton Gang might best be described as opportunistic criminals, not deputy marshals. Yet here was Frank Dalton's name.

Questions arose...

Was he somehow related to the famous outlaw gang? Though there were more and more families moving west during the latter part of the 19th century, this was still a small and distant corner of the country—the border of what was a rapidly receding frontier. He must be related.

I was intrigued. Yet that word does not seem to capture my future fascination.

And Frank Dalton's life was lost in the line of duty. It seemed to me that any memory of him was lost as well—yet there was his name on a cardboard marker, so he wasn't *completely* forgotten.

My fixation with Frank Dalton began there. The memorial had served its purpose exactly. That said, I could hardly memorialize a man I knew nothing about. There was no memory there to draw upon for remembrance. And so, I began what has become something of a quest.

The questions haunted me. Who was he? What happened to him? If Frank was a member of the illustrious Dalton family, why isn't his story as memorable as that of the outlaw brothers?

The last question, of course, is rooted deeply in our American psyche. That we celebrate outlaws is nothing new. The practice is as rampant today as it was in the late 19th century when journalists who'd never stepped foot in the West penned lurid hyperbole that immortalized criminals like the Daltons.

This simple cardboard placard reminded me of an injustice I've always felt. Frank's life and death is buried in obscurity. That didn't seem right. I wanted answers. For me. Maybe for Frank.

Some of those answers proved easy enough to find. Frank Dalton was the elder brother of the outlaw Daltons. In fact, some of the outlaw brothers had previously ridden with him as his posse and continued as deputy marshals even after Frank's death.

Through all my digging, though, I couldn't help but feel like Frank Dalton's life was positioned as a footnote in someone else's story. He's reduced to a paragraph in most of the outlaw narratives. His death becomes an episode in the local legends surrounding Judge Parker's Court. And for the Marshals, who identify Frank Dalton as part of their extended family, his name is one among many—those who made unimaginable sacrifices in the name of a much larger cause.

In the early 2000s my son, Sam, became a park ranger at the National Historic Site in Fort Smith. By this time, I'd roped him in on my research efforts. With his inside access, Sam found handwritten transcripts of the investigation into the Dalton death in 1887. Sam, my wife Susan, and I began to transcribe (and, in some cases, translate) this lengthy document. The effort served to provide primary source material for my inquiries into the life and death of Frank Dalton, but also provided the foundation for multiple living history programs for the historic site.

The transcripts stemmed from hearings before the Western District of Arkansas Federal Court Commissioner. The testimony came from those involved in a deadly shootout and others at the scene. Unsurprisingly, some of the details provided by different participants didn't line up exactly. Some proved wholly contradictory.

Questions of motive aside, these testimonials do provide an accurate account of who was there at the shooting and when it happened. And as I dug deeper into Frank's biography, knowing the who and when of his final moments felt gratifying. The picture, such as it was in my imagination, began to coalesce.

Where, though, and *why* remained elusive.

In 2006 Robert Ernst published *Deadly Affrays*. Ernst had accepted a Herculean task—documenting the deaths of U.S. Marshals who had died in the line of duty. The first casualty, Robert Forsyth, was born in Scotland and one of the original thirteen marshals appointed by George Washington. He was killed in 1794 and Ernst's book chronicles the lives and deaths of 287 other public servants.

Deadly Affrays includes Frank Dalton. Mr. Ernst was often in Fort Smith, as too many of those deaths have ties to the Western District Court. I had the privilege of meeting Ernst on several occasions.

During one conversation, I asked him how he took conflicting versions of an event and came to a conclusion. The testimonials from hearings into Dalton's death—my best window into the events of Dalton's last day—were still troubling me.

As a law enforcement officer, Ernst noted, he applied his expertise to determine the most logical scenario. This is the root of critical thinking, a trait that seems sadly antiquated today. Even with critical thinking, our interpretations can be imprecise.

My understanding of Dalton's death, the ultimate version I'm presenting in this book, varies, at times, from that of Ernst and other published accounts. In my conversations with Ernst, he pointed out that his book could not go in depth in every one of the 288 cases he documents. He also indicated that he appreciated our research into the details of the Frank Dalton case.

I've researched every available version of the shooting. *Deadly Affrays*, after all my digging into this shooting, remains the definitive version in print.

That said, in the last few years, I've discovered more of the story. The big questions that are left are the why and the where.

My professional training is not in the field of history. My wife and I both became registered nurses in 1972. I first started working at Sparks Hospital while in high school in the 1960s. Most of my career was in inpatient psychiatry. I headed up the psychiatric units for more than twenty-five years. My wife worked at the same hospital her entire career, but in many different roles–in neurosurgery, the Emergency Room and finally as head of Education.

Upon my retirement from nursing, I decided to find out where the shooting took place. While Fort Smith in the late 1880s was reasonably well documented (owing, in no small part, to its notorious court system), the other side of the Arkansas River remained wild, and this has led to wild speculation about where Frank Dalton met his end.

Though the testimonials clearly state that Dalton rode a short four miles away from Fort Smith, researchers continue to speculate that the shooting may have happened much farther up the northern bank of the Arkansas River, near Van Buren, Arkansas, or deep within the floodplains of Paw Paw Bottoms—an area that's little more than an Oklahoma ghost town now, thanks to the recurrence of flooding.

The effort of finding the locations of the shooting has been hampered by the inadequacies of hand-drawn maps. Roads have moved. Bridges have been built. A railroad that bridged the Arkansas immediately after the shooting is just as distant in our collective consciousness as the shooting itself. All of the testimonials place the shootout in a very specific and named place on the Oklahoma side of the river, but where—exactly—has faded from living memory.

To find the spot, I enlisted my friend and history buff Al Drap. Al and I had worked together on history projects before, and I understood how much he could contribute to our quest. An architect with an eye for detail, Drap seemed to be the perfect choice.

In addition to his grasp on local history, he also knows how to read a map. His resume includes research for Art Burton on Deputy Bass Reeves and research on locating this area's route for the Butterfield Stagecoach line.

We started with the clues in the testimony. Deputy Cole states it happened "four miles from the city." Four miles as-the-crow-flies, or on what passed as roads in the shifting flood plain?

Various other references point to "the bottoms" and "the river." Parts of the Arkansas side of the Arkansas River have immovable stone bluffs. Try as it might, the river has failed to cut into this side, which is why Fort Smith exists where it does. Just upstream, though, and downstream, and all along the Oklahoma bank, the river sometimes goes where it wants, making these geographical markers somewhat malleable.

Deputy Cole clearly indicated that the shootout happened within the Cherokee Nation. While this might seem like a large target, it isn't in this area. The tribal allotments belonging to the Cherokee and Choctaw come together along this bank. Eliminating the Choctaw Nation's lands allowed us to narrow our search.

These clues led us to begin looking in the Arkansas River bottoms north from what is now Arkoma, Oklahoma.

The directional "four miles from the city" remains problematic. Four miles, yes, but starting from where? Our assumption for a deputy in 1887 would be the Federal Court House. These men were paid by-the-mile, so had fixed starting points.

If you stay along the river to the southwest, you will eventually get to the Arkoma Bottoms. Going north along the river will take you into what was Cherokee land, and on to Crawford County Arkansas.

So we began by going south, in Choctaw territory, four miles along the northern (or western, depending on its orientation) bank of the river.

We were looking for a connection with the testimony that the shooting happened in "Payne's Clearing." We could not locate anyone who had heard of any landowners named Payne. While this area is sparsely populated today, we still couldn't find anyone who knew of the Dalton killing.

This area was Cherokee land in 1887 and the records from that era continue to prove elusive. Our search then moved to old maps and lots of conversation. The testimony indicated that several houses, a small community in fact, existed where the shooting took place. The only community that we could locate in the area roughly four miles away is (or was, if I'm honest) a tiny town called Paw Paw, Oklahoma.

Paw Paw no longer exists. Like much of the history of this area, Paw Paw was washed away by the river. Evidence of where it stood in the 1800s does still exist. There is an immaculate cemetery that is well cared for and an old school site that is little more than a stone foundation in the dense canebrake.

Could it be possible that the location of the Dalton killing is now underwater? The U.S. Corps of Engineers channel project in the 20th century deepened the river but did not extensively change its course. Though it remains hard to nail down definitively, the current river's course appears to be very close to the same path it cut in 1887.

The riverbank in Fort Smith is in the same place now that it was back in 1887. Paw Paw's was established sometime around this time. As the Arkansas River runs between these two points, we have two fixed points of reference for the river's course.

But our cursory explorations of this area still felt like a stretch. Paw Paw is approximately ten miles from Fort Smith, not four. The most optimistic takeaway from Paw Paw was our logical conclusion that, even with the Arkansas River's voracious appetite, a flooded-out community can still leave some trace of itself.

Just south and west of Fort Smith lies the community of Arkoma. Here, the border between the two states isn't determined by the river. Apart from the abused signage and the sudden proliferation of check-cashing establishments, there's nothing to differentiate the poverty that straddles both sides of the line.

But Arkoma slides downhill into wide wetlands and tributaries on the southern bank of the Arkansas. We scoured maps and satellite imagery of the opposite bank and couldn't find evidence of a site across from Arkoma.

This is how searches go. We hadn't found Payne's Clearing, but we'd found where it wasn't.

After how long, and how many miles, and how much coffee–probably a good year or so? A lot of these roads are poorly marked farm roads. Many are on private property. It was never clear if we really should have been there. We did not see a lot of other people.

Most modern farming in this area is done by a few people on huge machines. When we did see someone, either a gas field worker or occasional farmer, they were always nice and seemed interested in what we were doing. When we occasionally got stuck on some nowhere backroad, someone would stop to help. None had ever heard of Frank Dalton, but would often say, "You need to go ask so-in-so."

Eventually, Al had to follow other pursuits and we agreed that I would continue the search on my own.

Standing on the Fort Smith side of the river—the high side—I could look across the expansive bottom lands on the Oklahoma side. I could see where the shooting took place if I only knew what to look for. I had no idea where to continue looking and began to despair that I had come to a dead end.

My obsession with locating the site, though, remained.

After running through all the geography, I turned to genealogy. Where were the illusive Paynes of Payne's Clearing?

My sister and her husband–Laura and Monty Thompson–gave me a history of Sequoyah County. My brother-in-law's family has deep ties to this area. This record listed some Paynes, but none of their stories seemed to mesh with Payne's Clearing.

Even without an exact location, I'd come to believe that Frank Dalton died in what is now Sequoyah County, Oklahoma. Sadly, though, Payne's Clearing–the little community where the shooting happened–seemed to have vanished before any of the chroniclers of Sequoyah County picked up their pens. Maybe even before the county was a county.

The search, such as it was, had played out. I resigned myself to the realization that this, too, would remain another piece of Western history shaped as much by legend as fact.

I needed a break.

I got one from an unexpected source, Judge Isaac C. Parker–well, his court records anyway.

Fort Smith is still a small town. Newcomers often comment on how the locals all seem to be related, somewhere down the line, and that's just how it was in the 1880s. The evidence I'd needed came from the historical record of a completely unrelated court case. Finding the Paynes seemed like the best way to find Payne's Clearing.

Combing contemporary historical documents turned up two brothers, Gabriel and Houston Payne, who operated a ferry from Fort Smith to the Cherokee Nation At last, I had not one, but two suspects for the Payne's Clearing connection.

With these names in hand, I approached Shelley Blanton of the Pebly Center at the University of Arkansas–Fort Smith. Blanton, a consummate researcher, proved to be a great resource.

With the tie to Paynes on the Fort Smith side of the river, Shelley quickly produced a wealth of information on others in the Payne family. Much of these leads came from 1800s newspaper accounts. Very little information appears in recent historical sources.

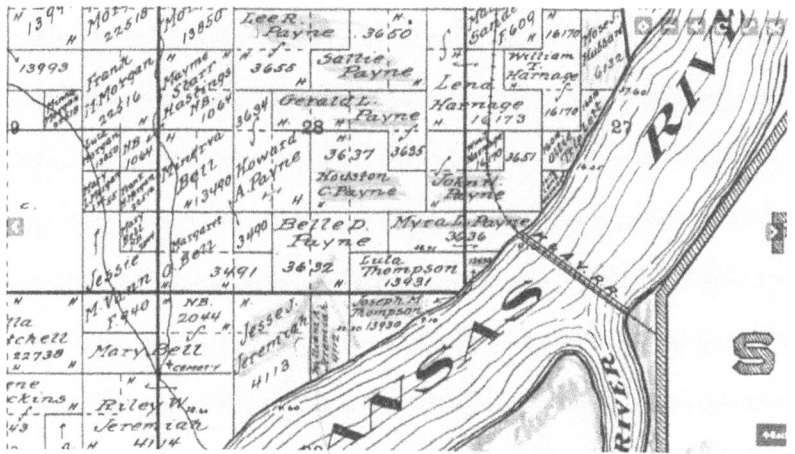

Cherokee allotments in Indian Territory across from Fort Smith

In short order, an argument developed that Gabriel and Houston are the Paynes from Payne's Clearing.

1. These Paynes owned a sawmill across from Fort Smith. Payne's Clearing was a lumber cutting camp.

2. The Payne brothers owned property across the river that is consistent with the area identified in the testimony—well within the limits of a true four-mile radius of the Fort Smith Courthouse.

3. The testimony says, "Payne's Clearing near the Cook Lease." If you were a non-Cherokee, you would have been required to lease the land. Since Payne's Clearing is not identified as a lease, it is likely that the Paynes were

Cherokee. Genealogical research shows that ole Gabe and Houston do have a strong Cherokee lineage.

4. The final and most important link is a reference in the testimony to a Payne house. A further examination of the handwritten testimony clearly shows it to be "Gabe Payne's house."

Finding houses from the 1800s isn't difficult in Fort Smith, but very little survives the floodwaters on the Oklahoma side of the Arkansas River. Only one house dating to the 1800s, to my knowledge, still stands.

Could that house be the site I was looking for–Payne's house, built on what had been Payne's Clearing, from lumber cut at the Payne's sawmill… This seemed to be a long shot.

I was able to locate the present owners of the house. Could this really be happening? Had the Payne house been sitting there for the whole time?

Despite having more than ninety thousand residents, Fort Smith still has a small-town feel. I put out some feelers and asked around, seeing if anyone had any connections to living Payne family members, or to the house on the far side of the river. And it didn't take long.

I was standing in Yeager's Hardware store when my phone rang—a call from the owner of the house.

The current owner—now in her eighties—had just the piece of evidence I needed. She confirmed her husband's family had purchased the house from the Payne family. Better yet, she had contact information for the Payne descendants still living in Fort Smith.

Jerry Payne, a Fort Smith native, agreed to meet in Oak Cemetery at the graves of his ancestors Gabriel and Houston. In that family plot, along with Gabe and Houston, were generations of their descendants. Jerry kindly provided me with a photo of his father, who was born in the Payne house.

Was the Payne house on the site of what once was Payne's Clearing?

Jerry was a wealth of information about his family's past—but only the history that occurred in the 20th Century. Beyond that, though, there were scattered stories.

Not a one of those stories included Frank Dalton.

Yet Jerry was able to provide one more clue that would prove invaluable. When asked about Payne's Clearing and the informal community that had sprung up there around the logging operation, Jerry was sure it still exists.

Houston and Gabriel's mother was named Martha Ann Moffett Payne. Moffett, Oklahoma, a derelict town at the foot of the highway bridge that now crosses the Arkansas River, was named for her family.

Payne's Clearing might just be Moffett, Oklahoma.

What was once Payne land is now Moffett. The evidence here is beyond dispute. But tidiness can often prove distracting to historians looking for easy answers. Moffett is not quite far enough, as-the-crow-flies, to be "four miles from the city."

On the roads that exist today, Moffett is just over a mile from the courthouse.

The Garrison Avenue Bridge (historically known as either the *Million Dollar Bridge*—for what it cost to build it, or the *Free Bridge*—for what it cost to cross it), connects these two communities. The bridge spans the river on the north side of Fort Smith's fort and empties into Moffett.

If Moffett or the Payne house was the site of Frank Dalton's death, we'd need to account for the proximity to Fort Smith, and the testimony clearly states the shooting took place four miles from town.

There are two equally plausible explanations. The first is an idea I picked up from Dave Kennedy at the U.S. Marshals Museum; deputies, being paid by the mile, might not have been the most accurate source for the reports on their mileage. Padding seems to be a common practice. To be fair, gauging mileage was an inexact science in the 19th Century.

My own theory is that these deputies were measuring mileage like we might today, especially when their destinations might have been in sight of Fort Smith. Yet there was no bridge in 1887. The most direct route taken to reach what is now Moffett in 1887 was prone to being washed out by the regular floods of the Arkansas.

Another road from the ferry led away from the river. This necessitated that travelers cut over about a mile onto more stable ground before cutting south toward Moffett. And then to ride east, back towards the river, to get to Payne's Clearing.

Mapping these old routes would require an archaeological survey. Some of those roads still exist, though they've been paved. The others have been lost to time–given up when bridges were built.

After several years on this quest, I feel that I've significantly narrowed the radius of possibility for where Frank Dalton met his tragic end. I do not know exactly how far the clearing, the site of the shooting, was from the house. This is not the end of the search, but it is where my search has led me.

Sketch of the 1880s Payne House

* * *

The original working title for this book was "Where did we lose the good Dalton". I was telling my son about the book when he proposed "Finding the Lost Dalton" He was right. His title is shorter and more succinct. It also changes the fundamental approach to the subject matter; the search moves to an area much broader than just location. When he said, "Finding the Lost Dalton," I knew that I had been looking for more than just the location of Deputy Dalton's death–I was trying to find the essence of the man as well. Thanks son.

I should not have been surprised that his title would be so much better than mine. After all, he is a far better writer than I am. He routinely amazes me with his ability to store a vast numbers of facts in his brain. My contributor said of my son "If he is interested in something, he knows everything about it and if he is not interested, he knows nothing about it." He was spot on. It is through my son that I found a contributor that makes this book possible. They have been friends and collaborators for years. They make an impressive team.

A few years ago, editor Dave proposed that I write a review of a reproduction of a historical firearm. That was my first real attempt in many years at writing. I agreed on the condition that my son would help me. Any father relishes the chance to do a project with his son. When the piece was published, my son surprised me with a forward that gave me credit for his long-standing love of history. I was blown away. These guys keep me humble.

All of the above is to say how I came to the realization that I was looking for much more than the geographic spot where Deputy Dalton was killed. I hoped, along the way, to find Frank himself. I want our subject to be more than a vague shadow. I long to know something of his character and substance. How do you build a ghost of history back into a flesh and bone man. I realized I had no chance of doing this from the 21st century, I had to find my way back to 1887.

The idea was to put Frank in context, to understand his time, to try and conceptualize the place he chose to make his home and bring his role as a deputy to life. All I knew to do was look everywhere I could think of to find our lost Dalton. Did we find him? I know a lot more than I did for sure. Perhaps you can never really find anyone lost in the dust of history. Maybe it is not even about the finding, it could be about caring enough to look.

Sallie Payne, wife of Gabriel Payne

The Dark Year of 1887

There was plenty of darkness to go around in the 1880s Fort Smith, Arkansas. Even the town's nickname was horrific: "Hell on the border." Just which part of Fort Smith was so hellish depends on who you ask.

Those on the wrong side of the law had reason to cast aspersion on Fort Smith—those that lived, that is. Hell on the Border's most infamous legal authority had earned a grim moniker: *The Hanging Judge*.

It is unclear how prevalent these colorful epithets were during the heyday of the jail and court, but they accurately reflect the conditions in the justice system during that era. And Fort Smith still marked the western edge of the border, even though America as we know it now had already begun to show across the continent, and much farther west.

As troubling as The Hanging Judge's justice process was, capital punishment was not the only source of the gloom hovering over Fort Smith.

Those tasked with upholding the law were dying, too. It went even further than the death of Deputy Frank Dalton. His killing is but one in a long line of death. Dave Smith and the Dixons were gone quickly, but the aftermath of these events reverberated in that family for generations.

An nineteen-year-old Will Towerly gunned down two of seven Deputy Marshals killed in the line of duty that year. All seven killed were in the area of what was to become Oklahoma. 1886 held only two recorded deaths for the Marshal's Service, and 1889 five.

The killing of deputies went on for years. Most were concentrated in a small area of Indian territory roughly the fifty-mile radius around the Cherokee capital of Tahlequah, making it the deadliest area for law enforcement deaths in

United States history. Even in this murderous era, the bloody year of 1887 stands out.

Dan Maples...

We lost deputy Dan Maples that year too. Like Frank, memory of Maples has receded in the wash of history. Most are familiar with the twentieth century legacy of bootlegging, but running liquor was commonplace, and, like Dalton, Maples became a casualty of the illegal whiskey trade in the Indian Territories when he was ambushed and killed.

Who shot Deputy Maples? That has never been satisfactorily answered. Multiple books have tried. I would propose that Maples' death resulted in one of the strangest and most controversial man hunts in law enforcement history when the focus landed on Ned Christie as a suspect. I say manhunt, but there was never any dispute as to where Christie was. He simply stayed home and dared the Marshal to try and get him. More and more came for him over the years. Christie eventually built himself a fort and finally was killed at his home without ever giving testimony or going to trial.

Whoever you believe Maples' killer was, there seems to be no dispute that he was killed by a Cherokee. The shooting happened in front of numerous witnesses, right in the middle of the Cherokee capital.

Even as I write these words, I run the risk of appearing to be anti-Cherokee. That is not my intent—or the intent of my contributor who has Cherokee roots. Several books have been written about the case and its aftermath. Almost all of them are from the Cherokee perspective. Yet there is another viewpoint that has been mostly neglected—that of the deputies who sought to bring justice for their fallen comrade. They have a side to tell as well, however complicated this story becomes by the clash of cultures.

The justice system was, is, and probably always will be flawed. I consider it to be the epitome of a necessary evil. Capital punishment, the role of incarceration, jurisdictional rivalries..., these have always been part of our society and likely always will be. That doesn't mean we shouldn't debate their merits and flaws.

All of this and much more descended like a landslide onto this small area of the west in 1887. Somehow all the boulders seem to fall onto this one single case of Dan Maples. Volumes have been written about the question: was Ned Christie an innocent man persecuted and killed because of his Cherokee identity and beliefs?

A simple core belief of our society remains (however theoretical) "innocent until proven guilty." Ned Christie was killed by deputies before he could have his day in court. As such, he will always remain innocent of the crimes of which he stood accused.

What would have happened had Christie stood trial?

Any attempt at an answer would be nothing more than speculation. Christie, when faced with the choice of arrest or a life on the run, chose to run.

He was pursued for years, but never left the Cherokee Nation and never made a statement about the killing—other than his repeated protestation of his innocence.

The argument that is commonly made in his defense is that Christie did not believe he could get a fair hearing from the United States authorities. This was a legitimate concern in 1887, and for many still is today.

I can admire Christie's position on Cherokee sovereignty, and his belief in preserving the traditional ways of his people. For me, though, I see another side. Christie put his family in jeopardy when he made his stand for his beliefs.

If one man can defy the law, for whatever reason, are we not left with anarchy?

Christie fought the good fight. The marshals sent posse after posse, and he fought them all until the last.

I personally doubt that Christie killed Maples. Bud Trainor is a better suspect in my view. Trainor was also a Cherokee. Trainor, though, was not a Keetoowah or traditional part of the tribe. This group opposed the intrusion of federal authority and the attempts to break up tribal lands. Trainor was likely not very political, and there's scant evidence to show he was associated with the traditional faction of the Cherokees.

Trainor did come to Fort Smith and submitted to an interrogation. Even so, he was never charged with the murder of Deputy Maples. Why not? We may never know. There is no good record of all the cases that were not charged. There are multiple theories: he may have been rightly seen as innocent, he may have turned state's evidence, or he could have been too well connected to have been charged. All of these, though, are only speculation.

It is hard for me to see what—if anything—the Cherokee Nation gained from any of this. It is clear, yet often not stated: Deputy Maples was a real hero.

Bass Reeves...

The final chapter in the tragedies of 1887, at least for the Marshal's Service, remains the trial of Deputy Bass Reeves–the first black Deputy U. S. Marshal west of the Mississippi.

Reeves stands out in American history. He was born a slave in 1838, yet by 1887 he had amassed a fair amount of property for himself and his family. In the reconstruction era that followed the Civil War, blacks were given the chance to make their place in society (on paper, at least) and Reeves certainly did just that.

But by 1887 things began to regress. In Fort Smith, Marshal Carroll, a former Confederate, was appointed.

Like many of us, Reeves' past wasn't spotless. In 1884 Reeves shot and killed his cook while out on the trail—an incident that Reeves characterized as an accident.

The story is that Reeves was cleaning his gun when it went off. If this was the case, Reeves' actions were wholly negligent. Cleaning a loaded gun is, for obvious reasons, dangerous—as is pointing a loaded gun at your cook. Guns don't fire themselves; at the root of any negligent discharge, as these incidents are labeled today, is *negligence*.

Reeves explained, and most of his contemporaries accepted, that the incident had been an accident. Reeves had immediately given medical aid to his employee. Despite his culpability, Reeves was not charged with a crime at that time—in 1884.

That changed when the new ex-Confederate Marshal came to power.

Carroll charged Reeves in 1887. Reeves was acquitted. Though legally cleared, he lost everything else he had. His farm went to pay for his defense attorneys, and he quickly left Fort Smith and his job. He separated from his wife, too, and moved on.

Reeves later took a job as a deputy out of the Texas District, and finally as a city police officer in Muskogee where he worked until his death in 1910. Reeves never seemed to recover from losing everything in Fort Smith.

One point often missed is how the Constitution of the United States helped Reeves. The Constitution in all its wisdom, created the separation of powers with three branches of government: Legislative, Judicial and Executive. When one branch failed Bass, another came to his aide.

This is exactly how the Founding Fathers meant for checks and balances to work. The authors of this document did not envision helping a former slave, but they did none-the-less.

The Marshal's Service, including the appointed Marshal like Carroll, is part of the Executive Branch. These positions are appointed, though, and not elected. This makes the position political by nature, leaving it (at times) open to abuse.

It is unclear if Bass held this view. He testified in his own defense and maintained that the shooting was accidental. I am not aware that he ever commented on the unfairness of his being charged in the first place, but he was clearly affected by it. When his own Executive Branch failed him, the balance was righted by the Judicial Branch in the person of Judge Isaac C. Parker and Reeves' ultimate acquittal.

As the trial unfolded, Marshal Carroll had difficulty making his case. The prosecution's best witness was a man that had been arrested by Reeves. It would appear that Judge Parker was not impressed by this witness or his testimony. When the witness finished, the Judge—not the defense attorney—called up a witness from the spectators present to refute the character of the prosecution's witness.

Lawyers assure me this never happens and is not supposed to happen. The testimony shows clearly that the Judge was unconcerned about his own impartiality and was going to help Bass. This additional witness is only identified as "Auntie," but her contribution was classic. No attorney asked her any questions, only Judge Parker. He established that she knew the last witness well. He then asked her if he had been in prison.

"I don't know if he was in prison," Auntie replied, "but he sure was gone for long periods of time."

The aspersion on the man's character was enough. Bass won his case.

Over and over, many sources–including the honorary tombstones placed on many of the deputies' graves in the 20th century–make what might seem a trivial error about our deputies: They rode for Parker. While I understand the utility of this shorthand for the era and location we are covering, the statement is simplistic and its usage erroneous. Saying that these men "rode for Parker" does disservice to the Marshals who served and, too frequently, gave their all. They were Deputy Marshals, not deputy Judges. If they were riding for Parker, they got off in the wrong branch.

A bad year—a worse job...

It is hard to overstate just how impossible the job of Deputy Marshal was in this time and place.

On the face of it, this kind of law enforcement seems simple; a crime is committed, and the Marshals find the suspect and make an arrest. Of course, it has never been that simple, but the realities of working on the border was way beyond complicated.

If you did manage to find the suspect in the thousands of square miles of hostile territory, in spite of language and cultural differences, you may not have been allowed to arrest him. If anyone involved in the crime is Native American, the tribal police could claim jurisdiction.

Even if you have arrested the right person of the right race for the right crime, you may not get paid unless you've brought the right paperwork.

There was no salary, no retirement plan, and no benefits. You would get a fee only when you brought in a prisoner, alive, for which you had a writ.

Marshals were paid for their travel, though the fee schedule was ridiculous. Marshals were paid one rate going out, and not paid coming back. As cliché as it sounds, they were paid another rate if the creeks rose. Even for a government system, the absurdities stood out.

Deputy Marshals furnished their own equipment—wagons, horses and supplies—and were responsible for provisions for themselves, their prisoners, and any assistants they hired. These assistants, posse members and camp cooks, were employees and the U.S. Marshals had no responsibility for them.

Anything a Deputy Marshal's posse did reflected on him, even if the Deputy Marshal was not directly with them. If his compensation was iffy at best, these posse members took an even greater chance of not getting paid.

Deputy Marshals were out often weeks at a time, in the open, in mostly undeveloped and hostile countryside. They had to make their way through a maze of rules and laws, sometimes to find they were under an investigation for their expenses. The Western District, in size and scope alone, made it stand out from the other districts. Irregularities in expense reporting led the federal government, on more than one occasion, to send investigators to the district. These investigators, most of whom were unfamiliar with the territory, had the power to dismiss anyone they accused of fraud. That could end a lawman's career.

Then there was the ever-present violence. Hunting up fugitives in the Indian Territory meant Deputy Marshals stayed out on the trail for extended periods of time with prisoners that were wanted for a variety of crimes, including murder. But they still had to camp, and camping requires gear.

Some of that gear, like the ubiquitous axe, could be dangerous in the wrong hands. After what could be weeks on the trail, Deputy Marshals and their employees were bound to let down their guard at some point. There are two documented cases of guards being killed by prisoners who managed to get control of axes.

A trip through Oklahoma today seems tame by comparison. While the western half of the state is arid and can be brutally oppressive in summer's heat, the eastern half of the state consists of low rolling hills, wooded mesas, and the subdued beauty of the Ouachita Mountain range.

But Hollywood has painted a picture of The West that looks more rugged.

The 1969 film *True Grit*, a story set in Fort Smith, was filmed in Ouray County, Colorado and Mammoth Lakes, California.

In 2010, when the Coen brothers remade the film, they chose to set much of the action in Santa Fe, New Mexico and Texas.

But far more deputies lost their lives in the less cinematic area surrounding Fort Smith than any other place in The West. Tombstone and Deadwood pale in comparison. The total number of deaths in this neck of the woods numbers more than fifty.

Why anyone would even remotely consider this job remains beyond my comprehension. But they did, some two hundred of them, but that number is hard to pin down. I asked Dave Turk, the historian for the U. S. Marshals service, how many Deputies were in the field in the Indian Territory at any one time. He indicated that it was a problematic question because so many of the deputies were "Special Deputies" who were employed for a specific task only. My best guess is the number of deputies at one time numbered about twenty. These are the men who kept going out, even when about one-in-four never made it back.

End notes...

The primary source of the continued family trauma for the descendants of the survivors of the tent shooting is the writing of Darrell M. Hume, *Tragedy Stops By*, published in Oklahombres Winter 1966.

The best reference for Marshal line of duty deaths remains *Deadly Affrays* by Robert Ernst.

Ned Christie, by Devon A. Mihesuah, is by far the most scholarly work on the Dan Maples shooting. It is, in my view, a continuation of the Native American perspective on the incident. This book devotes itself to the idea that a Cherokee is wrongfully accused of murder, yet Ned is still depicted as a viable suspect. There were others at least as suspect and possibly more so. Since Ned would never submit to a trial or even an interview with federal authorities (or Cherokee officials as far as we know), this will always remain an open case and a question of who-done-it.

The author mistakenly accuses the wrong Cherokee of a different murder. Mihesuah writes that E.C. Boudinot killed B. H. Stone in Tahlequah, when this was more likely his brother William Boudinot. She does point out in the notes that there is no case file for the murder, so E.C.'s brother is only a suspect since no charges of murder are found in the files.

She also claims E.C. was a supporter of Nationalists like Christie when he was clearly on the opposite side. This all comes up in her rationalization of why the Cherokee Chief stayed out of the Christie case. She argues that the two murders of white men in the Cherokee capitol would have put the Nation at risk if the Chief had supported Christie.

This may be a reasonable supposition but there is no evidence provided to support it.

The book *Black Gun, Silver Star* by Art T. Burton is the definitive source on Bass Reeves. Burton's *Black, Red, and Dead* is also informative.

I recommend *The Lawmen* by Frederick S. Calhoun for an overview of the Marshal Service. *Forging the Star: The Official Modern History of the United States Marshals Service*, by David S. Turk is also essential reading.

A Brief Chronology of the Arkansas River

The Arkansas River isn't as storied as the Mississippi River, nor does it loom large in the nation's psyche, like the Rio Grande River. The river runs for 2,364 miles, through four states, and carries the snows of the Colorado Rockies down to the Gulf of Mexico. And it runs through the pages of this narrative—both the historical events and our current search.

Much of what we know about the river and its valleys comes from studies of regional geography. The river has been following a similar course for thousands—some say millions—of years. Its history predates the European explorers who would first chronicle, cartographically at least, the river we know today.

In 1541 Francisco Vásquez de Coronado's expedition found Etzanoa—a thriving city in what is now southern Kansas. Etzanoa fell to the spread of European disease and would disappear. Archaeologists believe they've located the site and have recently begun excavations.

But those groups were hardly the first. The archaeological record shows that ancient civilizations relied on its waters more than a thousand years ago—Mississippians in the east and the Anasazi in the west.

Before that, nomadic hunter gatherers found prey in the wide floodplains and left their exquisitely crafted spear points as evidence. We know little about the Clovis and Folsom groups, and next-to-nothing about a migration that unspooled over thousands of years.

Gaps in the historical record shouldn't be read as evidence that this history never existed. Much of the knowledge of history and culture that we're missing today were once the province of oral history belonging to families and tribes that dissipated under the weight of Manifest Destiny.

The loss of oral histories is still transpiring—a problem we face in our search of these banks for anyone, even two generations removed, that can help recount details of Frank Dalton's murder.

In 1673, Father Jacques Marquette, a Jesuit missionary, and Louis Joliet had set off down the Mississippi. The pair was acting on behalf of France, looking for a navigable water route from the Great Lakes to the Gulf of Mexico.

They made it as far as the mouth of the Arkansas River, and there they met the Quapaw.

This was a contentious era in European politics, and those politics were playing out in the territories. The Quapaw were hospitable and assured them that the Mississippi did flow unencumbered to the Gulf. The two explorers had a choice—continue down the mighty Mississippi, or head back north and report their findings.

There were some Spanish folk farther south, the Quapaw reported. They had traded with them. So, our intrepid French explorers decided they'd gone far enough and went back north.

This would be a brief footnote for the Arkansas Region, except the name Marquette gave the region stuck. Like many place names in this country, Arkansas began as an honorarium for the people who lived in the region—the Quapaw—phonetically transcribed in French as Akansea, then anglicized again and again until the spelling was standardized as we now know it.

But the French, politically at least, were not long for the region. They sold their interests and focused on more pressing matters back home. They left their mark, culturally and linguistically, on the headwaters of the Mississippi and the spreading delta at its end.

The United States, though, and its territories, continued their westward spread. And the Spanish claimed the area south and west of the Arkansas river, at least through some of what's now Colorado from 1819 to 1846.

During this time, the Arkansas ran unencumbered. And the native populations along much of its length were further stressed by the intrusion of gold miners, ranchers, and farmers from the east.

No chronicle of the Arkansas River's history would be complete without an acknowledgement of the role the river played in the forced relocation of the Cherokee, Choctaw, Creek, Muscogee, Chickasaw, Seminole, Quapaw, Illinois Confederation, and others.

Duplicitous treaties, pandering politicians, and a population explosion on the east coast led to unfathomable cultural upheaval and atrocities that are beyond the scope of this text—though they will play an interesting role in the death of Frank Dalton.

Much of this path, what's become euphemized as "The Trail of Tears," follows a portion of the Arkansas river. What would, by the 1830s, come to be known as Indian Territory— the land set aside for the groups that were driven from their ancestral lands like cattle—sits in the Arkansas River Valley.

Today, as you cross the Arkansas line on Interstate 40, the landscape changes. The fertile fields east of Little Rock—an area now dedicated to rice production—rise into the foothills of the Ozark Mountains. Across the state line, though, those mountains are replaced by long mesas—a geological phenomenon more common in The West than The South. The tall trees begin to shrink in the arid winds that blow in from the prairie to the north. The wastelands that fill the rangeland is now home to natural gas rigs and wind turbines.

This area would have been uninhabitable if it weren't for the river. The Arkansas runs much of the width of Kansas before turning south and irrigating a wide swath of eastern Oklahoma.

In the 1890s, the river's potential for agricultural use was heavily exploited. The Arkansas River irrigated vegetables and orchards in Colorado, then wheat as the river left the mountains, and during the hottest of the summer months, it ran dry. Played out.

From the time of forced relocation, through to Oklahoma's statehood in 1907, the Arkansas was only a river part of the year. Summers, without it, must have been brutal.

Water rights remain a contentious issue along its course. A series of dams have made more of the river more consistently navigable, yet these dams have altered the seasonal flood patterns.

In Fort Smith, the Arkansas makes a wide horseshoe shape that defines three sides of town. The river runs east but approaches town from the west, then hits the stone bluffs on the edge of downtown and turns north. Along this brief stretch, the river forms the border between Arkansas and Oklahoma.

On the northern bank from Fort Smith, Van Buren sits in constant danger of floods. That town has dikes along much of its length. The river, though, cuts back to the south before turning east again and running to Little Rock, and eventually to the Mississippi River.

Back in Fort Smith, the river was once the defining feature of the town. The original fort was built high on a stone bluff, its guns overlooking the river.

Economic development in 19th century Fort Smith was fueled by the river—and the city thrived. The Federal Court that sets this story in motion was at its heart.

Unlike some cities that spread out from their geographic centers, Fort Smith then—and even now, to some extent—grew cramped against the eastern shore. The river was the literal border between what some residents perceived as civilization and savagery. Fort Smith was the United States, except when it was briefly part of the doomed Confederacy.

In the 1880s, The West of America's collective imagination was certainly wild. The romantic paintings of Remington and Moran, and the iconic photographs of O'Sullivan and Jackson showed landscapes and people that captivated

Americans back east. Yet the people in Fort Smith were there.

While the lands in Indian Territory were less dramatic than the granite domes of California, or the jagged peaks of the Tetons, those living in Fort Smith had only to cross the river to find frontier.

Fort Smith is a transitional space. It is important to note that this space between the cultures, between the national identities, between the landscapes is not a simple line, the river provides definition—the boundary. That it wasn't easy to cross (unless it had run dry), helped keep the transitions clean and easily identifiable.

Yet by the 1880s, when Frank Dalton began riding for the Marshal Service, this wilderness, the frontier, The West, was rapidly growing in American mythology, but shrinking in reality.

Very few of these rivers were left to be explored. The blank spots on the maps were filling in. The Spanish were gone. Mexico had stopped pushing north. Americans had pushed north along the western coast all the way to the gold fields of Alaska.

Yet the inner-mountain west was still wild. Natives, ranchers, cattlemen, missionaries, miners… all of the iconic and solitary cliches that would come to define the era of Manifest Destiny…, they were spread across the continent. And they were just across the river.

After the Civil War, Fort Smith was an American city. Across the river, though, it was still wild.

* * *

How should we honor the memory of the deputies who gave their lives in the line of duty? I think any attempt to keep their story out there has value. Here in Arkansas, we have a stretch of highway called the "True Grit Trail." As far as I can tell, there is nothing but the sign. I suppose it is hard to commemorate a totally fictional event.

Right outside of the Fort Smith National Historic Site (a truly noteworthy museum) is a mock front old west town where Hollywood style gunfights are staged—the extremes of historical remembrance.

I applaud all efforts. Here is my effort to find the truth, the grit was already there.

Indian Territory Deputies

We all have an idea of what law enforcement does, either from what we have seen in the media or personally experienced. Much of what we think we know doesn't apply to the Indian Territory deputies.

It may be helpful to start with dispelling some common misconceptions.

Myth 1 The police should patrol to prevent crime. The territory for the deputies was almost seventy thousand square miles. There were likely no more than fifty deputies at a time—maybe as few as twenty-five. You do the math.

Myth 2 Traditional patrols, since they were United States Marshals, could go anywhere in the U.S. The country was divided into districts, A deputy was supposed to stay in his district and leave other districts to the deputies assigned to that district.

Myth 3 A Marshal was a policeman. Remember Matt Dillon? The Marshal was an administrator, the Deputies did the police work.

Myth 4 Once a deputy found a criminal, he could arrest him. An arrest could happen if a Marshal observed a crime themselves, but this was discouraged. The main task for the deputy was serving precepts. Someone would make a complaint that a crime was committed, and typically name who might be involved. Then a precept was issued, and a deputy was assigned to serve it.

So, if it did not work the way we may have thought it did, how did it work?

The deputy was appointed by the Marshal of the district. The Marshal was appointed by the President every four years. The deputy had to be reappointed each time. New Marshals likely meant new deputies.

Deputy U.S. Marshal Frank Dalton

In the territory there was not a system of law enforcement, town marshals, or sheriffs etc. The Indian Police took care of Indians in their nation only, everything else was the responsibility of American deputies. The deputy marshals made their income, before the 1890s, by fees paid only if they brought in someone they had a precept for.

Some of the appeal of being a deputy was the status of the position. He was a federal officer. This was considered a step up from being a local officer. Many of the deputies had previous experience in some other law enforcement capacity. It was not uncommon for someone who served as a posse man or an assistant to the deputy to move up the line–at least to make deputy. It would have been unusual for a deputy to make marshal since this was mostly a patronage job.

Did integrity count? This was all up to the marshal. Much has been written about the idea that having a criminal background would be an asset when looking for crooks. Not all deputies were upstanding. It is equally unfair to say that they were all crooked. There is no definitive record one way or the other that I am aware of. Some deputies, a minority, made a decent living. I do not know of any that got rich by nefarious means or legitimate ones. It is my view that most served honorably.

There was no uniform, not even a standard badge. Few pictures exist of a deputy who wore a badge. The one seen most often with a badge is Coon Ratree. With a name like Coon, and his appearance, he may have needed a badge to convince anyone that he was a deputy.

The standard appearance, in photo evidence, is a deputy in a white shirt, a vest, and a suit coat. We have been conditioned by western fiction to picture them in the field looking like cowboys. Deputy was a step up from the cowboy, and they dutifully dressed the part. Add to your suit, a Colt, Winchester, and an open crown wide brim hat and you have the deputy look.

When you rode out of Fort Smith to serve your writs you took your posse man and cook with you. These were the only assistants that you had. You hired them and trusted your life to them. The cook was also the guard for your prisoners. In a lesser role than yours, they may have only had a shotgun.

On your journey into the too dusty or too frozen territory, you took a wagon. Do not picture the typical movie jail wagon. A jail wagon was only used at the Fort Smith jail. On the trail the wagon of choice was a typical open farm wagon. Some reports say simple modifications like rings to chain prisoners to the wagon had been added. I think even this was unlikely.

At least one tent was often used, probably for the deputy, with most everybody else sleeping under the stars. This was a more casual affair than you might expect. Testimony shows that families of the prisoners sometimes came along for the ride.

If the deputy chose, he sometimes let prisoners show up for court on their own. The number of prisoners collected varied greatly, depending on the luck of the deputy. You were looking for a suspect, with no picture, no address, and no limitations on what name they chose to use. How did they find anybody?

It was the deputy's responsibility to feed this crew. A limited budget and lack of refrigeration on the trail posed obvious problems. Cooking was done over an open fire. You could expect lots of beans and potatoes. Baking soda was on the list of supplies, so some form of bread was included. I can picture a Dutch oven by the fire. Still, this wasn't just another camping trip; you might get killed by your fellow campers.

When you got back to Fort Smith, it seemed everyone was trying to make a buck off of the court system. Your arrival back with your load of prisoners always made the papers. The court business was big business in Fort Smith. The wall around the jail compound was lined with vendor stalls. You could get tamales or roasted peanuts. There was one booth where a deputy could sell any gun he had confiscated, even though he was supposed to turn them in and receive nothing.

When he got to the courthouse steps, there was a gauntlet of lawyers yelling for the attention of potential clients. This would occasionally deteriorate into a barrister's competitive fist fight. Lawyers, right?

When your suspect made it to court, the evidence, such as it was, would be presented. Fingerprints, DNA, ballistics, trace evidence, mug shots–none of these were available to the court. In the case of Jack Spaniard, convicted of killing a deputy, the most compelling evidence presented was the fact that a dog at the crime scene looked a lot like Jack's dog. There were no eyewitnesses, but a deputy was killed. Jack was not known to be an upstanding guy, and that was often all it took.

In another case forensic evidence was offered. Deputy Cap White testified that he knew the killer fired from inside of a cabin. When asked how he knew, Ole Cap said "someone" had told him if you took your handkerchief and rubbed it on a log (the log of a log cabin) and the hankie was blackened, that was from gunpowder. Forensics had to start somewhere.

An eyewitness was by far the best the court had. Fort Smith could be hundreds of miles from the home of the witness. He was dependent on the court for his subsistence while waiting for his turn. 1887 was not only bad for the deputies, but the witnesses as well. Congress had failed to appropriate funding for these witnesses, so some four hundred of them were stuck miles from home, and in most cases, with nothing to even feed themselves. Once again, this history confounds belief.

* * *

Sitting at the end of Fort Smith's main street is a statue of Deputy Marshal Bass Reeves. He is depicted as a heroic figure astride his horse, well-armed, facing west, ready to head out and defend us all.

I am proud of my community and my small contributions to this monument.

You may have noticed that statues have taken on notoriety as of late. There is no evidence that Bass ever owned slaves, he was in fact a former slave--quite a neat departure from most of the monuments found in the South. Makes me proud.

Making a fitting tribute in bronze is not an easy thing. For one thing it takes money, usually contributions from a broad support base--civic support, and government as well. You also have to take into account the vision of the artist for the piece. Bass's statue includes a faithful dog. In an early meeting with the sculptor, I pointed out it was a dog that almost got Bass hanged. The artist said he wanted the dog. It may be ironic, but it is a cool dog.

At the other end of the street facing in the opposite direction are three smaller statues. One is a 19th century supporter of Fort Smith schools, and one is a nun. I suspect there are not a lot of nun statues. She is there to represent the Sisters of

Mercy, the cornerstone of Fort Smith's health care system for more than a century now.

The lead statue does not sit on a horse. He sits in a chair, the other two are standing. I don't know if anyone else has contrasted the two sitting figures. But they do bookend the two branches of our Justice system. Someone has to be riding out to whatever destiny holds while the other one sits in the chair of judgement. Judge Isaac Parker was not a slave holder either, in fact he fought to free the slaves—will that be enough for his statue to escape scrutiny?

The Courtroom

Judge Parker was an improvement over the guy before him–Judge William Story. Faint praise I know. Story left the bench in disgrace, agreeing to resign to avoid prosecution for fraud. The corruption in this era ran throughout the Fort Smith community and all the way to Washington.

Judge Isaac C. Parker

Isaac C. Parker took over the impossible job and ruined reputation of the Western District of Arkansas in 1875. His district was half of what we now know as the state of Oklahoma.

In 1871 alone, Judge Story convicted 37 men of murder. Not one of them was executed. Only seven men were hanged for their crimes during Story's time on the bench. Punishment was not easily avoided in Parker's courtroom. In his first year he hanged five men simultaneously. He was just getting started. Systematic fraud ended with Parker.

It is difficult to judge the Judge from our modern perspective of proper justice. We have come to take for granted all sorts of forensic evidence, fingerprints, ballistics, DNA, etc. None of these things were available to the courts. There was not even any reliable way of identifying anybody.

You were literally whoever you said you were.

The task Parker accepted was to bring as much justice as possible to what was in effect a totally lawless land. He had a great deal of sympathy for the tribal nations who were the likely targets of much of the crime. His court was honest and hard working. It took its toll on him. Were good intentions enough?

An objective evaluation of a 19th century judicial system is always a challenge. Limits to the evidence available at this time, as well as an impossible case load have to be taken into account. Parker had to find a way to make this work. A study of his directions to the jury do not correspond to what we 21st century critics find acceptable. However, when you consider what little evidence was available, his directions that clearly showed his bias towards conviction become at least a little more understandable. This may have been justified if it was effective in curbing crime.

Unfortunately, there is no objective data that it affected crime rates. Another criterion for evaluation is the courts responsiveness to the victims and non-criminal users of the system. By keeping all the functions of the federal court in Fort Smith, and not closer to the people of the Indian Territory, Parker made an extreme hardship on the innocent who needed his court. The horseback travel was time consuming and psychically difficult. Parker had the power to make commissioners all over the Indian Territory, making it much more efficient but he would not do it. Instead, he insisted on personal control. The final point of evaluation is the Judge's ability to keep up with the times. Legal standards change and they certainly did in the late 1800s. Parker did not seem to see this. He became increasingly out of touch and lost many cases to appeal towards the end of his career. After 1889, the appeals went to the Supreme Court.

In conclusion, I believe you have to give the court a mixed review at best. Honesty and hard work get an A. Flexibility and fairness to all get a D.

When the Federal Court did what it was supposed to do..., what was it supposed to do? A hell of a lot. What helped create the one-of-a-kind caseload was the lack of a territorial court and law enforcement system that every other territory was given. Because this was Indian Territory, the various Indian Nations were given the right to form their own judicial systems. This was a well-intentioned idea, and mostly worked within each tribe. However, what fell outside of their jurisdiction posed some unique problems. The tribal courts had no jurisdiction over non-Indians. It is fair to say that the non-Indians caused the vast majority of the lawlessness. The jurisdictional dispute this caused has never been solved.

Most of the crime in the territory involved liquor in one way or another. The federal government decided all alcohol was illegal in the territory. This alone would likely overwhelm the judicial system. Hanging was the mandatory sentence for murder or rape until 1897. Add in counterfeiting, forgery, postal crimes, and anything involving government property. What exactly was government property was often in dispute. Generally, the Federal Government believed it had control of most everything in the territory.

The court also had civil issues to deal with. As more whites flooded into the territory, railroad claims and corporate issues also came to dominate the court's time. This was just in the territory. And there were riverine issues, bankruptcies, bigamy, incest... At various times the court also covered large areas of the state of Arkansas for federal issues. Judge Parker, with the backing of congress, decided he was the only one capable of doing all of this. He was going to do it all himself or die trying. He died.

End notes...

Indian Territory and the United States, 1866-1906 by Jeffrey Burton

A Shovel of Stars, By Ted Morgan

Isaac C. Parker by Michael J. Broadhead

I am aware that this is not, strictly speaking, your traditional history book. I am sharing some of my personal journey. This is not something I do very often..., you probably don't do it much either.

It feels like an odd thing to do. It's not like I have something special to impart. If it works at all it is because you may see something of yourself in me. Writing a book has been a very real struggle for me. It is fraught with questions. Should I? Can I? Will anyone care? Sometimes in the middle of the night the demons grow pretty big...

Notes from May 23, 2022

Our hunt for the site where Frank Dalton was killed remains an ongoing saga. Even today, as we put pen to paper, we continue to make attempts to contact anyone that might have information relevant to this book.

Early in the summer of 2022, I called the current owner of the house that I believe to have been owned by Gabe Payne. She kindly connected me to the current occupant, a woman who has lived in Moffett, Oklahoma since she was a child. Her grandfather was the Mayor of Moffett, and she is the current Mayor.

She told me she has been the keeper of Moffett history since she was 20 years old. She is now 62. She also recounted that the house is a love story.

It was built by Sam Houston Payne for his Cherokee wife, Martha Ann Moffett. The town of Moffett, Oklahoma is named for her family. They settled there, across the river, because Payne felt he couldn't bring her to Fort Smith. I assume at this point it was because of the prejudice of the era.

Martha is buried in a Cherokee cemetery in Tahlequah, Oklahoma. This, though, was a time of cultural change. The couple's sons—part Cherokee—are buried with their Cherokee wives in Fort Smith. I do not know where Sam Houston Payne is buried.

I exchanged a couple of phone calls with my new source in Moffett.

Here is someone just across the river from me with more pieces of the puzzle. They may not even be pieces to the puzzle that I am working on, but nonetheless they are a part of history.

This house stood high and dry for more than a century, but a flood in May of 2019 changed that. The Arkansas left its banks and the flood deposited mud up to your knees in the Payne house.

This current resident promised to go into her attic at the Payne house, the attic where she'd stashed decades worth of photos, documents, and artifacts and see what she was able to salvage that might be relevant to our search.

She, being of a like mind, grasped instantly what I am hoping to do with this book, which is to save this story and get it down on paper before it is lost in the mist of the past.

At the same time, I have finally been able to get an appointment to look at the paper files at the Fort Smith National Historic site. Covid, staff shortages, and maintenance issues have delayed this for a couple of years.

But this is 2022. Loren McLane, the park historian, sounds eager to assist me. Shelley Blanton at the Pebley Center at UAFS continued to help fill in gaps in my research.

All of this—the new leads on the ground in Moffett, the continued support of archivists and academics—makes me feel somewhat under water. I'd thought I was almost done with the search.

Two much better historians than I could ever pretend to be, Tom Wing and David Turk, both told me to not fear new information but to embrace it, even when it proves what you were sure you knew to be wrong.

That is great advice.

This story is expanding and continues to bring out other interested sources.

At this point I don't know what I don't know. What is in the attic, the files, or cyber space? We shall see.

I wanted to record this in real time because I wish I had done the journaling of this search early on. It never occurred to me that the search itself might be of some interest.

When I did start writing this stuff down and proudly showed it to my contributor …this seems a good time to mention my contributor.

Once I realized I might have found a few of the answers to this historical mystery, I realized that I had no idea how to write a book. I needed some big-time help.

Fortunately, my contributor lives around the corner. Dave has taught writing all over the country for years and now makes a living as a writer. I was beyond delighted when he agreed to come on board.

He does not have the time and I do not have near enough money to pay him what he is worth.

When I gave him one of my first attempts at writing this, he took it and began to cut it into small sections. As gently as he could, he said "all of this is good and we need to include it all but on this one page—in probably two hundred words or less—you have gone in seven different directions."

He was right. My mind has a tendency to pinball. Dave says everyone does, but you can't write a book that way, or at least not a readable one.

This brings me to the point I am trying to make. Yes, my manic brain is scattered all over, but so is history. You never get the whole picture. You only get tattered crumbs. Try to make something out of that. Good luck.

Honestly, I get so excited when I find something. Here's another clue—where does it lead?

All of this is to say that right now, in the summer of 2022, I have to see if this tangle of new information amounts to anything. Hopefully something interesting and coherent. I must be about four am, I needed to get this down on paper. Here's to hoping you can empathize.

* * *

Once I realized that the search had to be more than just a patch of dirt. I had to find the story that tries to tie it all together. This is about real people, they had lives, and it is my job to find as much as possible about them, or all I would have is a dead piece of ground. So begins our tale in 1887.

Analysis of the Shooting

Most books that cover the "Dalton Gang" at least mention the killing of Frank Dalton. Frank was the eldest brother, and a role model for Grat, Bob, and Emmett Dalton.

In my view, much of what has been written is questionable. References are generally sparse. I suspect most references go back to Emmett Dalton's writings. Emmett claims his source of information about the killing of Frank comes from the surviving deputy James R. Cole. But it isn't that simple. Deputy Cole shared his account of Frank's death with his brother Bob Dalton. It was Bob that then shared the details with Emmett.

Such word-of-mouth can have deleterious results. Emmett's third hand account was recorded fifty years after the event and would, in that era, be almost impossible to verify. But the version recounted by Bob Dalton could have happened since Bob Dalton was a deputy marshal in the same area and at the same time as Deputy Cole.

One can conceive that if your brother was killed you would want to hear directly from a deputy that was there, and that you might have a vested interest in retelling the story.

The other sources for Emmett's version of the story? Despite some word of mouth, and although not often credited, the contemporary newspaper accounts would have shaped his understanding of the events.

The killing was widely covered but these reports vary greatly. Even the date of the shooting is often incorrect. This rampant inattention to detail goes as far as the incorrect date on Frank's tombstone.

One source of material that is rarely cited is *The Proceedings before Commissioner Brizzolara*. These testimonies and proceedings began two days after Frank Dalton's death.

This material has not always been available and was handwritten by the court clerk. I have not found that a transcribed version of this document has ever been published. It is in the appendix of this book. I hope you will evaluate it for yourself.

It is the position of this author that this sworn testimony remains the best primary source available on this event. However, there are multiple witnesses. Each brings a slightly different perspective. Some may have likely had their own agenda. As such, some interpretation of the evidence presented would seem to be prudent. I will try to note why I believe my version of the events has merit.

There are two written versions of the killing of Frank Dalton that are worth special note.

One is the book *Deadly Affrays* by Robert Ernst. In my opinion this book relies too heavily on Deputy Cole's version of events. But it does not fall back on often erroneous sources like some interpretations do.

The second version comes from Darrell M. Hull, a descendant of another victim in the shooting whose writings appear online at genealogy websites. His essays have appeared in a couple of historical journals and have evolved after he was able to include new information from the Brizzolara proceedings. Mr. Hull's subsequent writings are studied and insightful. He acknowledges that he includes oral family history in his work. Also, he is open about his emotional attachment to this material. This does make it subjectively more difficult to evaluate.

These two versions do not universally agree, nor do they always agree with my interpretation.

Hull and Ernst do make compelling and well researched cases for their conclusions. Both sources are currently difficult to find but are worth the effort.

With the above being said, here is what I think did or did not happen.

1. *Deadly Affrays* is an almost word for word account given by Deputy Cole and agrees with Cole that it was Mr. Dixon that shot Cole. The problem with the descendant Darrell Hull's account is he uses unverifiable oral family history that Cole was Frank's deputy. But both Frank Dalton and James Cole were of equal standing. Both were deputy marshals. This means both were on equal footing going into the camp.

2. Almost universally, previous publications claim that the deputies were looking for three bootleggers. In fact, testimony clearly indicates that the deputies were looking for one man—Dave Smith.

The earliest source I have found for the multiple-criminals-theory is Emmett Dalton's writings. I believe he inflated the number of shooters to make his brother Frank appear more heroic.

3. How many "outlaws" did the Deputies face in the shootout? They only had writs for one man. Each had a writ for Dave Smith. There is no official record that they were aware of the second gunman riding with Smith—Will Towerly.

There were multiple adults and children in the tent where the shooting occurred. Did any of them get involved in the gun fight? Despite Cole's testimony to the contrary, no other witnesses could verify that Leander Dixon or his wife was also shooting. In my view the Deputies faced only two shooters.

4. Who shot Deputy Cole? This may be the most disputed part of the incident. The witness testimony appears to clearly show that Deputy Cole shot both Mr. and Mrs. Dixon when they ran into the midst of the shooting.

Deputy Cole is the only witness to state that he faced a threat from Mrs. Dixon. Cole also claims he was shot by Mr. Dixon.

It is my view that Deputy Cole was defending his own actions. When asked, the other witnesses stated they never saw Mr. Dixon with any kind of weapon.

Except for Deputy Cole, all the witnesses agree that there were only two men shooting at the deputies—Smith and Towerly.

Deputy Cole had killed Dave Smith before he was wounded. That leaves Will Towerly as the best suspect for shooting Deputy Cole.

All three possible shooters of Deputy Cole (Smith, Towerly, and Mr. Dixon) died before they could face charges in court, so there will never be a definitive conclusion.

5. Who did Deputy Dalton shoot? In *Beyond the Law*, Emmett Dalton states that "Dixon and Smith were both on the ground, each hit by one shot from Frank's gun."

The testimony does not support this. No one could verify that Deputy Dalton fired even one shot, much less two shots that hit two men.

Deputy Cole killed Smith, Mrs. Dixon, and wounded Mr. Dixon. On the other side, Smith wounded Deputy Dalton and his associate Towerly likely wounded Deputy Cole and ended the killing at the site by shooting the wounded Dalton.

6. When did this all happen? Various dates have been reported, but the testimony is clear. November 27, 1887—the Sunday after Thanksgiving. It is significant that it was a Sunday because this was an active lumber cutting camp. If it had been any other day, everyone would have been out working. Because it was a Sunday, there were multiple witnesses. And there were also multiple victims—some of whom may have been bystanders.

7. Who is at fault for the deaths? This is how I would rank each of the participants.

Starting with the most culpable (a) Dave Smith. He was the only wanted man. His actions, and his proximity to Fort Smith, mocked the system and brought the Deputies to a tent full of men, women, and children. He fired the first shot.

(b) Will Towerly. There is no report that anyone was looking for this nineteen-year-old. Towerly was riding with and was a follower of a wanted criminal. He likely shot Deputy Cole and clearly executed the wounded and defenseless Deputy Dalton.

(c) Deputy James Cole. I can't fault him for shooting Dave Smith in the back after Smith had shot his partner, Deputy Dalton, but Deputy Cole made the situation worse when he shot Mr. and Mrs. Dixon. These two may have been innocent. The only word against them came from Cole's own self-serving testimony.

In Cole's defense, this was a running gun fight. Cole's partner had been shot and Cole was wounded, and he continued to receive fire from the tent.

However you decide to judge Deputy Cole's actions, he retreated for cover, shot two additional people, and left before all the shooting was over. While wounded and under fire he may have fired at anything.

But he was the one who survived.

(d) Deputy Frank Dalton. Dalton rode blindly along with Deputy Cole into what turned into an ambush. It is doubtful that there was any way for either of them to have foreseen this. But that is what happened.

Unlike Deputy Cole, Dalton may have hesitated before firing. He never fired a shot during the entire fight. Dalton was the first down and wounded.

(e) Mr. Leander Dixon. Leander Dixon was likely unarmed. No one suspects that he shot anyone. But he did run into the middle of a gunfight. To his credit, this was reported to have been an attempt to aid his wounded wife.

(f) Mrs. Jenny Dixon. Jenny Dixon used questionable, albeit understandable judgement when she ran into the middle of the fight to help her wounded and dying brother.

(g) Dave Smith's father-in-law, John Pearson. Knowing Dave Smith was a wanted outlaw, Pearson still told Smith where to find Smith's wife, Lizzie, at the lumber camp.

(h) The Pearson couple. The Pearsons were there, with their children, in the tent with a known criminal, Dave Smith. They did run once the shooting started, and their actions may have saved the children.

* * *

My drive to tell a story that might interest you is fueled by a lifetime of western movies, television and books. The area and time covered here is the same Charles Portis covered in *True Grit*. I love that book, not to mention the two movies (three if you count the John Wayne sequel—which I do). All of it is so good. It is exactly the way I want the real history to be. The romance, the excitement—you know what I mean. If life was half as fun as fiction…Then again, maybe it is.

The Event

In 1887 two Deputy Marshals, Cole and Dalton, unknowingly rode into a shootout. Some would call it an ambush. Only Cole would ride out. Frank Dalton would die in the dirt along the Arkansas river in the Indian Territory.

The two had joined forces the night before. It was a quiet morning in late November, the Sunday after Thanksgiving.

They took the time to eat their breakfast before riding a short distance over to a lumber camp. They were both looking for the same man, Dave Smith and only Dave Smith.

He had given no indication that he was hiding from the Deputies. He was riding around openly in the camp.

Law enforcement had been alerted when Smith ordered a jug of whiskey from across the river in Fort Smith. Smith likely knew this might draw attention to his location, with Fort Smith being the seat of law enforcement for the territory. But it happened, and Cole and Dalton knew right where he was.

It was quiet in the logging camp. The log sided tent held seven adults and three small children. The deputies had no way of knowing who was inside the tent.

There was a terrible surprise waiting. Smith had a partner in crime—a second gun. He was just a kid of nineteen but still proved to be a deadly adversary.

You never know how these things are going to start. The beginning of this day could not have been more ordinary. It was a small community of other tents, but mostly houses. It was Sunday morning so most everyone around was home including our tent dwellers.

Dave Smith was holding his infant daughter on his lap, where he usually kept his Winchester. Meanwhile his wife Lizzie went outside the tent to get more bread. She found much more than fresh biscuits—two well-armed deputies were approaching. She gave a warning to her husband which gave him time to swap his baby for his rifle. Things heated up rapidly.

Cole and Dalton rode into the clearing. The sawdust had piled beside the now silent steam powered sawmill. As they neared the tent and dismounted, the smell of sawdust was cut by the warmth of bread baking on the campfire.

As Cole approached the back of the tent, Dalton went to the front. Dave Smith wasted no time, he stepped from the tent, his Winchester in hand and shot Deputy Dalton before he could fire a shot. With this one shot, Dalton was already out of the rest of the fight. Deputy Cole then fired the fatal shot into Smith's back. The one man they were looking for was now gone. The fight could have been over, but panic seemed to rule the day.

The quiet stillness of the Sunday morning was replaced by gunfire, gun smoke, and horrific screaming. Dave Smith's sister ran to him. This was not a wise choice. As innocent as it may have been, Cole shot her, too. The toll was already three and was still mounting. Her husband ran to her, and he was shot and wounded.

Chaos. Who was doing the shooting? Deputy Cole shot Dave Smith and shot the couple that ran into the middle of this gunfight. But someone else was still returning fire from inside the tent—and one of those shots grazed Deputy Cole's chest.

Wounded, the deputy retreated from the tent to behind a tree. Amid this retreat, he ran past his wounded comrade. Cole called out to Dalton, but Dalton never spoke nor moved. As the shooting continued, Cole saw his chance to escape. He assumed his partner was in fact dead already, so he ran for his horse and rode back toward Fort Smith.

Back in the clearing, Frank Dalton was not dead. Not yet. He rose up on all fours to face a kid who had emerged from the tent. The Deputy begged for his life. At this point the kid faced a choice, ride away free or continue the killing. He shot the wounded deputy not once, but twice in the head, ending his life. Then he rode away.

End notes...

This is all taken directly from the testimony given in the investigation of the shooting that was conducted a few days later. There are multiple witnesses who testified from different perspectives. Some, the surviving deputy and Dave Smith's wife, likely had their own motives.

There were also witnesses with no apparent bias. When you have a multitude of witness stories, it requires an author to choose the most plausible version of events. This is always a debatable conclusion.

The testimony is available to the reader in an appendix. This is the first time to my knowledge that it has appeared in a book. The testimony is handwritten and took many hours and multiple people to transcribe. I stand by its accuracy. Every attempt was made to keep this narrative historically accurate.

At the same time within historic bounds, an attempt was made to place the reader into the middle of the shooting. Few liberties are taken, I cannot say with any certainty that the bread in front of the tent was biscuits. The people in the tent had Arkansas roots, so it is a pretty good guess. The testimony does not directly reference the gun smoke, just the gunfire. Guns of this era were still using black powder which is known for its smoke. It was replaced by a product known as smokeless powder, but smoke makes sense for this time.

Some things I considered including, but did not–blood, for example. With this many wounds you might assume there was a lot of blood and there might have been. No witness seems to mention the blood. Screaming yes, blood no. From my wife and my combined experience of more than ninety years working in hospitals, gun shots often do not produce as much blood as you might think. Not always the amount you see in the movies. So. blood is left out.

The other area that is tempting to address is individual motivations. A good example is the surviving deputy who left the scene.

The only one who will ever know his motivations is the deputy himself, and he never shared much on the matter. One might be tempted to speculate on what would have happened if Deputy Cole stayed in the fight. It could have gone one of two ways. He might have died. He did not describe his wounds as being serious, but the kid might have shot him, too.

From what I know of Deputy Cole, I would never bet against him in a shootout. He was the more experienced shooter and was better armed than his young opponent.

* * *

The heart of this book is looking for a place and a man. We have the place; the man has proved more elusive. It finally occurred to me that what I wanted to find was some old west romantic figure, like in the movies. I wanted Frank to be bigger and braver than life usually produces. I think he was just killed too soon. Deputy Cole on the other hand…well judge for yourself.

Notes for the Chapter on Cole

Ron Taylor is a good friend and retired Tulsa Oklahoma Police officer. "Some officers spend their whole career without ever touching their firearm," he said, "others retire with a long history of violence." Taylor helped us recreate the investigation of the Frank Dalton shooting. He was referencing his own personal observations, but they hold true for the 19th century, too.

There is no evidence that I know that shows Deputy Dalton firing his weapon in the line of duty. There is certainly no testimony in the inquiry to his murder that he fired a shot. Frank died early, at age 28 in 1887.

The other deputy in that shooting lived to be 80 and died in the 1920's. James R. Cole falls into Ron's second group–those with a long career of violence.

This chapter will address Cole's story, or at least what we know of it. It's fragmented at best. Trying to sum up a long life and career is never easy. Cole did not leave us much to go by, no journal, no memoir, not even an interview that I am aware of. What we do have is a couple of sworn testimonies from him, his very words. To have that is remarkable.

Of course, there was no ability to make a recording of him, so a written transcript is the next best thing. In my view, Cole just stuck to the facts. I think you can take this in one of two ways. First–this is what is expected when testifying, especially from a law enforcement professional of his standing. Second–Cole was all business. It is tempting to assume that Deputy Cole was the latter, classic hero stereotype. But the reality is we have no way of knowing what was in Cole's soul.

Take a look at what the eyewitnesses said about one single incident in Cole's life, the Frank Dalton killing. Picture with me from the actual testimony of what that was like, Deputy

Cole almost immediately had his only partner and ally wounded and out of the fight. He did not know if Frank was able to continue, what condition he was in, or if he was even alive.

Cole was alone in this fight for his life. Frank lay in the dirt bleeding. Then someone shot Cole. This wound wasn't fatal, and he continued to fight, shooting three people, but gunfire continued. Women and children ran out of both ends of the tent. The shooting continued. Again, what had happened to Frank?

The screaming stood out with the witnesses. I think anyone would conclude this had to be horrific. We cannot know what effect all this had on Deputy Cole. From our modern perspective, most of us want to say he had to have been traumatized. The hard reality is not everyone reacts the same to this type of situation. Some are not damaged but relish the thrill. This is not meant to portray either reaction as good or bad. They are different ways of relating to violence. What was the effect on Cole? I wish I knew.

Another issue in writing a profile of someone over a hundred years after the fact is trying to sort out the verifiable stories from the mist of rumor and myth. You can never pretend to do this perfectly. What we do know is that when Cole and Dalton teamed up for the fatal shooting that they had no way of knowing what was to come. Deputies typically had their own posse support system in place and did not join other deputies to serve simple writs. This certainly could have been a chance pairing and nothing more. That did occur at times. As for Cole's part there is a story, but not a verifiable one. Cole may have been alone without a posse because he had just been in another shootout where his posse man was killed. Like I say–I have been unable to verify this.

We know Frank was without a posse as well. It seems pretty clear that he often relied on his brothers, Grat and Bob. I do not know if Cole ever wondered how the shooting of Frank Dalton would have turned out if more of their usual support had been there. History fails to tell us where Grat and Bob were, or why they were not there. All we know is that the surviving Dalton brothers continued to work for the Marshals Service after Frank's Death, and eventually decided to try the other side of the law.

Deputy Cole's long life afforded him opportunities that Dalton's early death denied him. Little of Cole's personal life is known other than that he was married and had children, but what remains of his fragmented story is filled with more violence.

About a year before he was involved in the 1887 Frank Dalton shooting, he was in another shooting. Remarkably it was very close to the area where Frank was likely shot. Just like the Dalton site, this one was across the river from Fort Smith. Actually, right on the bank of the Arkansas–one more piece of evidence that a Deputy Marshal's life was in danger as soon as he set foot on the other side of the river.

This is a fluke of history for you; we know more about the man Cole meets on the other side of the river, than we know about J. R. Cole and Frank Dalton combined. We know his name–Spencer G. Rodium. His alias was George Spencer. He was from New York City, here to hide from a murder charge for killing a sailor. He worked as a farm hand and lived with the Mize family that owned the farm. He seemed to be the cliché dime novel western villain.

George Spenser was a bully, always out picking fights. He carried a pistol. "He was a rowdy fellow that flourished his pistol around a good deal. He was an overbearing man, and he would raise a fuss if he got a good chance," John Mize would later testify about Spencer. Miss Mollie Wyatt, another witness, intimated he had a crush on her or at least he hung around her house a lot. She was there when he got shot. Whiskey cocktail was Spencer's drink. Spencer thought, those who knew him reported, that the Deputy Marshals were looking for him but very likely he was wrong.

Prelude to a gunfight...

George was on the ferry returning from Fort Smith to the Indian Territory where he was living. John Mize had been with him all day and was a witness to the last. It is likely that this was Payne's ferry. Houston Payne, who may have been the ferry owner, was on the ferry. The Mize family land was just west of the Payne's property. It is this land we believe was known as "Payne's Clearing" and would be the scene of the shooting that left Frank Dalton dead and Deputy Cole wounded just a year later.

Most of the witnesses believed George Spencer to be drunk. He certainly had whiskey with him. He continuously harassed the other ferry passengers. Spencer reportedly took a whip from a wagon driver and began to swing it around. He was asked to stop, which didn't sit well with him.

Earlier in the day, Spencer had left his firearm in the engine house of the ferry for safe keeping while he went into Fort Smith, but decided he needed it now. Spencer began firing wildly, I suppose, to impress the inoffensive travelers of his questionable nature. As he reloaded, other passengers asked John Mize to load all the young ladies present into a wagon and get them off the ferry and out of there as soon as he could.

The Gunfight...

Cole was waiting on the western bank of the river for the ferry. As the boat neared land, someone recognized him and—perhaps goadingly—told Spencer there was a deputy on the bank. This was enough for Spencer to be ready to provoke a fight.

Cole approached the ferry as Spencer started to disembark. They both had their horses and were only about ten feet apart.

Spencer's first mistake was to threaten the deputy and demand he leave. He further pushed things by waving around his whiskey bottle and trying to get Cole to respond to the contraband.

If it weren't for the whiskey—in Spencer's bloodstream, not his bottle—he may have had an advantage. His gun was already in his other hand. Already cocked. Ready to fire.

What did Cole do? He stayed cool. He made every effort to diffuse the situation and told Spencer that he had no interest in him. But Spencer fired the first shot.

Most of the witnesses swore Cole had been hit in the mouth by the bullet. One said it was so close he saw the bullet move Cole's mustache. That's about as close as it gets.

But this is not the man you wanted to shoot it out with.

On the riverbank, ten feet apart, with their horses between them, Cole drew from his holster and fired almost immediately.

This isn't the typical wild-west shootout. Spencer fired at Cole, who was holding a horse with one hand, and drawing his weapon with the other. Cole reacted to the aggression from Spencer, recoiled from the aggressive action of the gun being pointed at him, and this likely saved his life. Spencer's bullet almost hit him. Everyone there thought it did.

Cole only needed one shot. He hit Spencer in the chest and the man fell. Spencer took his last breath, lying in the river sand, gun on one side and the whiskey bottle on the other.

Cole had almost been killed, then killed his assailant. Was he rattled? It did not appear so. He quickly and professionally organized the bystanders to deal with the scene. He ordered that someone take charge of Spencer's gun, and asked others to test the bottle to be sure it was in fact whiskey. He further took the time to explain his actions were not due to the whiskey violation but the need for self-defense.

The aftermath...

The shooting was investigated, and Cole was exonerated. This segment of our story is taken directly from the witness testimony.

One bizarre fact remains. Cole defended himself, right? He could in no way be held responsible for the shooting. He asked at the shooting scene if anyone would claim the body, and no one did. As strange as it seems, dealing with the body was all on Cole. This was a rule of the time. Cole loaded up Spencer's body, helped clean the corpse, provided a burial suit of clothes, and paid for the arrangements. Thanks for your service.

Yet another shooting…

I wish I could somehow fill in all the gaps between shootings. History has an unsettling way of only leaving traces of even the big violent events and nothing more. Cole's story is typical of this. I have found little of his personal life, can only guess at his routine duties as a deputy, and know nothing of the workings of his mind.

It is likely that this was the life of the late 1800's Deputy. A few newsworthy events over the course of years, and the rest just mundane everyday duty. This is probably still true today of law enforcement–flashes of excitement in a sea of routine.

That does not mean that the everyday stuff is not fascinating. It is just often lost over time. When you think about it, this is probably true for most everybody, a few memorable events and the rest is just a blur.

Which brings us around to the next shooting. Cole does not kill anyone this time, but another deputy did. Not only does his story intertwine with Cole's tale, but it also adds to our knowledge of what was happening in the Indian Territory in the late 1800s.

Here is how Deputy Cole is connected to this one. Cole had a posse man with the unlikely old-west name of West Harris. After serving as Cole's assistant, Harris had been promoted to Deputy and was working on his own.

One year before Frank Dalton was killed, Deputy Harris and Deputy Tyner Hughes had arrest warrants for two men. The two deputies and three posse men found their suspects four miles from what is now Blane, Oklahoma, in the Choctaw Nation, just south of where Frank Dalton would be shot.

Neither of the suspects was willing to go quietly, so—as the pattern of these events would suggest—the encounter turned bloody. In the shooting, both suspects were wounded, but none of the five lawmen were hurt.

It is always problematic to compare two different incidents. There are likely many different variables which we can never know—in fact we know much less about this shooting than we do the one in which Dalton was killed. All we can do is take the vague facts we are given and speculate on their relative importance.

Little is known about the Harris arrest covered briefly above, it is brief only because the recorded history of the incident is painfully brief. Could it have been the marked difference in manpower on the Marshal's side that allowed them to prevail? Can we draw any conclusion from random incidents? We can only speculate the reasonable conclusion that more manpower makes better odds.

But this wasn't the end of Deputy Harris's service as a Marshal. That would come in 1894.

Harris and his posse man, Frank Faulkner, had word that a man they were looking for named Charlie Benge was going to be at a party. Benge, Harris, and Faulkner were all Cherokee citizens. This was a Cherokee party at John Seabolt's house outside of Muldrow in Indian Territory. It is reported to have been attended by thirty to forty Cherokees.

The lawmen approached the house and soon spotted Benge, a former posse member himself, and a shooting erupted. I'm not being reductive with that description. No one knows why the shootout kicked off–we just have a lot of dead bodies, including Harris, Faulkner, and Benge.

When the report comes into Fort Smith, our man Cole was sent to investigate.

Your guess is as good as mine on what effect it had on Cole to see yet another partner dead on the ground. "He arrived

Saturday morning and discovered three bodies still lying in the front yard," Ernst writes in *Deadly Affrays*.

"Harris's pistol was still clutched in his hand and all the chambers had been fired," Ernst notes, chronicling the scene. "Benge's pistol was also in his hand, and it too was empty. Faulkner's gun was found about ten yards from where he lay; it also had been fired six times."

This was the other side of a deputy's identity–that of the investigator. Cole had to piece this altogether, and one element didn't add up. "Cole was struck by the unusual fact: Harris and Benge were killed with pistol or rifle fire," Ernst adds, "while the wounds to Faulkner indicated he had been shot with a shotgun, as well as pistol or rifle." But there wasn't a shotgun at the scene.

An almost investigation...

Cole tried; he really did. It would have helped to have advanced ballistics or fingerprints. Neither were available to Cole. His only hope, as was usually the case, was for an eyewitness.

Good luck.

The house owner was the only one to show up at the scene. Sure enough, he had been there, but he was too drunk that night to remember anything. And there was no indication of who fired the shotgun, or where that person went.

Deputy Cole looked for other witnesses. After all, there may have been forty people present. He could find no one willing to come forward. There were two more victims found, for a total of five people killed. Without witnesses, though, the case was never solved.

Deputy Cole put in a lot of years, but that is a lot of violence.

It's not over, though.

In 1896 Cole was still a deputy, having been sworn in for the third time. By this time, he had a more permanent assignment in Whitefield in Indian Territory. It was

Christmas. Everyone was celebrating. Well…maybe not Deputy Cole.

James Vault, a resident of Whitefield, chose to celebrate in the street with his friends and his pistol. Cole was against it. The gang of rowdy young men celebrating the holiday did not seem to relish Cole's interruption. It is unclear if Cole was already looking for young Vaught, or just wanted the revelers to settle down. One way or the other, their meeting went bad.

The group in the street closed in on Cole. What happened next is disputed. Let's just say Cole is not the man you want to crowd. He killed Vault in the struggle. Cole says the death happened accidently in the confusion; witnesses in the crowd testify otherwise.

Cole was convicted of manslaughter and sent to prison. But Cole was not without support. A judge signed an order for Cole's release after he had served only two months. Cole continued as a deputy and never went to prison again (or killed anyone else that we know of).

Why did this final shooting end so differently for the intrepid Deputy Cole? The best answer we have is that this time he shot someone that wasn't a known scofflaw. The support the young victim had from his friends and community did not play in Cole's favor.

Remember the Judge that released Cole from prison. It was H.H. Clayton from Fort Smith. Clayton had been a prosecutor in Parker's court. He undoubtedly knew Cole. He released Cole for the merits of the case, maybe, or because of what he knew of Cole, or maybe a combination of the two. As far as the record goes, Cole died peacefully in 1925.

End notes…

The main source for this chapter is court documents, found at the Fort Smith National Historic site. The Muldrow shooting's source is *Deadly Affrays* by Robert Ernst. Curiously he provides two different accounts of this odd incident. The account here attempts to combine them into one narrative. The essential story, Cole's role in it, and the victims stay consistent in all three versions.

The Ferry shooting adds to the clues on the location of Payne's Clearing, where Deputy Dalton was shot. We know from court records that the Payne brothers owned a ferry. The landing for the ferry on the Indian Territory side might well be near the location for the infamous clearing. "Payne's Ferry" likely landed at "Payne's Clearing." Stay with us here.

Since Houston Payne, one of the Payne brothers, was on the ferry, it seems likely he would use his own ferry. The other clue is John Mise was on this ferry. There was more than one ferry from Fort Smith to the Cherokee Territory. The roads on the territory side were notoriously unreliable, so logic would dictate that you would want to use the ferry closest to your destination. The Mise Land is just west of what we believe to be "Payne's Clearing." Granted, this is a stretch. This is not even close to the best evidence for our location theory, but it is a small piece to the puzzle worth mentioning. It is also intriguing that Cole was there at "Payne's Clearing" a year before Dalton was killed.

* * *

Bottom lands are strange places. At least they seemed that way to me. Once I realized that Frank Dalton's death site had to be lost in these bottoms, I started traveling through them. Of course, in Frank's time, the residents transformed these flood-plain forests to clearings–patchworks of small open spaces surrounded by thickets. Today the woods are just a fringe along the river. The bottoms themselves are mile-after-mile of endless rows, sometimes plants, sometimes just dirt.

I've spent many hours driving the farm roads. They are strangely quiet and desolate; it is rare to encounter another human. All the work now is done by huge machines that always seemed to perch abandoned miles away on the horizon. Occasionally, you would meet some lonely farmer or gas field worker. They never seemed to ask or care why we were there.

We asked whoever we met if they had heard of Payne's Clearing or Frank Dalton. No one ever had. Sometimes they would say "you need to ask [so and so], but they died years ago."

All you can do is keep going, hoping that the answer is in the next field or maybe the next…

Moffett -Exile across the River

Most towns and cities seem to have an area, usually an adjacent community, that has a questionable reputation, justified or not. Fort Smith has Moffett.

This is not to say that Fort Smith's reputation has always been sterling. Fort Smith, as the name implies, started as a fort. Soldiers are a ready market for all kinds of dubious recreational services. Bars and taverns sprung up just outside the walls of the fort and are still there, today.

This pattern continued for much of the 1800s, with a multitude of bars just on the main street alone. There was also an entire row of brothels on the Fort Smith side of the river throughout the nineteenth century. Sadly, only one remains (as a tourist attraction, not a working brothel).

And even after the soldiers left, the more questionable elements of the community remained. Well into the twentieth century, a squatters community existed in what is now a National Historic site.

Long before anyone thought of using the name Moffett, there was always a small settlement across the Arkansas river from Fort Smith. There were likely a few settlers on both sides of the river even before the soldiers came in 1817 to establish the first fort.

The fort was established to try and bring peace between the warring Cherokee and Osage tribes.

In the early 1820s an angry Osage chief and his band of warriors showed up at the Fort. You could tell he was angry–his name was "Raging Mad Buffalo." …if ever there was a moniker to strike fear along the frontier. Raging Mad Buffalo was certainly more fearsome than his predecessor Claremont.

The Cherokee didn't have names that we later came to expect of our war chiefs. They had John Jolley and The Bowl.

The White Man history does not put the Osage assault on the fort in a very favorable light. Their version indicates the Osage threatened the fort and demanded that they be bought off with black powder–a commodity in short supply for the Osage.

Black powder was not in short supply inside Fort Smith, a fact the soldiers demonstrated by rolling out a canon. The Osage fled across the river and killed some of the residents that lived in the future Moffett.

No one can say for sure exactly what happened, but I'd like to give the Osage more credit. It seems implausible that you make demands of a fortified location after telling them you were short on black powder.

Osage history paints a different narrative of the trip to the fort. Their arrival was meant to be a show of force. Black powder does not come up.

The Osage history doesn't dismiss the deaths on the western bank of the river. These settlers were intruders on their land, *so there*.

Whatever happened, Moffett had a bloody start.

Not all of Moffett's history is bloody. One of American history's most fascinating characters lived there: Sam Houston. This is the same Sam Houston of Texas Independence fame, and he lived there with his Cherokee wife.

At some point in the conflict between the Osage and Cherokee the Cherokee made their claim on what was to become Moffett. History records Sam's Cherokee wife as being named Talihina. That is a story for another time.

Talihina's sister appears to have laid claim to what became Moffett. Houston was drawn to the spot by his friend Captain Bonneville who was stationed at Fort Coffee nearby. The role both of these men played in the expansion of this country and their relationship with Andrew Jackson is, again, a story for another time.

The next time history points to blood on Moffett's soil comes in the civil war. Former slaves in the 11th Regiment of U.S. Colored Troops served in Fort Smith and were assigned to cut hay on Gunther's Prairie.

The exact location of this prairie has been another subject of speculation. Some place it about twelve miles northwest of Fort Smith. Since the Gunther name is closely tied to Moffett, I believe a good case can be made for the location of the incident being closer to our little community.

Five companies, some two hundred fifty or more men, were cutting hay on August 24, 1864, when Confederate troops found the black soldiers out in the open and attacked. Three of the soldiers from the 11th were killed.

A quieter time finally came to our little spot. Of course, this was only after the two-shootings covered elsewhere in this book. The early 20th century appears peaceful, even with Fort Smith's first airport being located there.

There was good reason why Moffett was not more developed than it was. Blood was not the only thing that was drawn to the place. If it wasn't blood, then it was mud. The Arkansas river was never kind to Moffett. Roads were built and rebuilt only to be washed away, decade after decade. It was only ever a matter of time before Moffett would once again be isolated and under flood water. This continues to this day.

During World War II, Camp Chaffee, on the east side of Fort Smith, saw a huge influx of troops preparing for the war. Like all soldiers, these men welcomed distractions from what was to come. Moffett was happy to oblige.

A small row of seedy bars became the hallmark of the town. Moffett's reputation grew. Almost anything could be obtained there, and the town seemed to embrace gambling and prostitution. The alcohol, as it had always done, fueled fights that sometimes ended in death.

The Army soon took notice and tired of sending the Military Police across the river to clean up the mess.

Moffett's next bit of notoriety came when it became the only town in the United States to be totally off limits to all military personnel. This elusive decree was believed to have lingered long after the bars were gone.

Looking at Moffett today, it is all but impossible to see traces of this debauchery. Much of Moffett has literally disappeared. Floods, neglect, and government ambivalence have all taken their tolls.

Still, a community remains. Moffett has looked for any way to survive–and they've had a few missteps. One survival attempt was a plan to raise needed funds through speeding tickets. It seemed to work too well. The state designated them "a speed trap" and dissolved the small police force. Catch a break? Not in Moffett.

Moffett is still there. Not exactly thriving, but still existing. There are a few bright spots. What some people would view as the less desirable business–a casino, a strip club and massage parlors–are now a few miles out of town. The town's stockyards and salvage yards have continued to be the only surviving businesses. Where the row of bars once stood, there is now nothing. The first new enterprise in years is a medical marijuana dispensary. The latest census shows the town down to a little more than three hundred holdouts.

Then there is the beautiful school. There are not enough kids left to support a school, but it's there. I asked one of the teachers how this worked, and she told me the school draws kids from all over the region, including Fort Smith. It seems the school has become a beacon for an outstanding reading program. A ray of light in an unlikely place. It's not all darkness.

End notes...

Fort Smith Little Gibraltar on the Arkansas by Edwin C. Bearss gives the historical view of The Raging Mad Buffalo incident.

The Osages by John Joseph Mathews gives the other side.

The Fort Smith *Elevator* September 16, 1904.

Did Sam Houston actually live in what was to become Moffett? The evidence is not the greatest. There is some evidence that he did reside there, albeit briefly. The best documentation is for his Cherokee wife's family owning property there.

It appears that they may have transferred the land to Dr. Payne and his Cherokee wife. It is her lineage that brings in the Moffett family name. References are scarce. The idea that Sam Houston lived there does help explain why Sam Houston Payne, a descendant of Dr Payne, was so named. Or it could be for some entirely unrelated reason.

The other clue that should be considered is the burial of Sam Houston's Cherokee wife at Wilson's rock, which is close to Moffett. Some will dispute that she was buried there, but most sources accept it. The best explanation for her burial there is that her family lived nearby and chose the spot near their home. The best case can be made for Sam Houston's Cherokee wife's [like many things, her exact name is disputed] family living in the future Moffett, and he probably did too until he could establish a more permanent base.

* * *

The search haunts me sometimes. You get invested in looking for answers, but that gnawing feeling of "what if there are none" is always there. Will there be enough? Did I look hard enough?

After the Dalton Killing

What happened to everybody after Deputy Dalton was killed?

Let's begin with the children who saw it all. Thankfully they all survived. With as much shooting that happened that day, survival was something of a miracle.

One of the children who made it out was Dave Smith's own infant daughter. Dave started this whole fight. When he did, he made a decision that placed his wife and child in danger. I can find no record of what happened to the baby or his wife. One can assume that the life of an outlaw's widow with a small child who was already living in a tent was likely not an easy one.

We do know that Joe Pearson was arrested and charged with Dalton's murder, however those charges were quickly dropped and should have been since there was little evidence to anything other than the fact that they happened to be there.

The Dixon's orphaned children Racheal (aged three) and Mathew (nine months) were taken in by a family in Van Buren, Arkansas. Their mother was killed in the fight. She was brought back by the same family that took in the kids and buried in a Van Buren cemetery. Exactly where the grave is remains unclear.

Lee Dixon, the father, was arrested for murder and jailed in Fort Smith, Arkansas. The only real evidence against him was the testimony of the surviving deputy, Cole, who claimed that Mr. Dixon had shot him.

Not one of the other witnesses seemed to have seen this.

Cole's testimony seems suspect in view of the fact that he shot the Dixons, both of whom appeared to have been unarmed. Within the month, Dixon recovered from his wounds. Even so, he died in jail, probably from malaria, before he could go to trial.

Dave Smith, the instigator of the shooting, who Deputy Cole shot in the back, lived for a short time after the shooting had ended. He spoke to his wife before he died from his wounds. She reported that he told her that if Deputy Cole had told him to surrender, he would have. This is dubious. A previous witness–one who appears unbiased–swore that Smith told him that if Smith had seen Cole first, he planned on killing him.

One could surmise that Lizzie Smith may have been motivated to try to shift some of the blame for all of these deaths away from her husband–the one who fired the first shot. It does deflect some of the blame from him, if you believe that all of this could have been avoided if he had been given the chance to surrender. Since Smith didn't survive to stand trial, all of this remains conjecture.

Deputy Cole survived. He has his own section of this book talking about what happened to him.

And Payne's Clearing, where the killing took place, also has its own section.

There is one other person left to account for–Will Towerly. This young man, likely only nineteen years old, rode into the scene of the crime with Dave Smith. There is no indication that either Deputy Cole or Dalton had ever heard of him. Cole in his testimony clearly indicates that they were looking for Smith and only Smith.

Many speculate that Smith and Towerly had been involved in prior criminal activity. Smith made no secret of his belief that deputy marshals would have taken him back to Fort Smith for hanging if they had gotten the chance. The charges against Smith were not hanging crimes. But neither Smith nor Towerly had the chance to explain their actions.

Dave Smith gave every indication that he preferred to shoot-it-out with the deputies he believed were looking for him. Could the same thing be said of young Will Towerly?

Although we cannot say for sure, there is some reason to believe that this was the case.

When Cole left the scene of the shooting, he had no idea who had been firing at him. With Cole gone, the coast was clear for Towerly to ride away and disappear. He did not. Instead, he deliberately and intentionally got Deputy Dalton's Winchester and approached the wounded Deputy with his own gun.

There was no reason to believe that Towerly was in any danger from the helpless deputy. Deputy Dalton begged for his life; the kid had a second chance to leave with no trace. Again, he did not. Instead, he shot Dalton in the head, not once, but twice.

Even at nineteen, he must have known the execution of a deputy marshal was going to put a big target on his back. Towerly finally decided to leave. Multiple witnesses though, had seen him shoot Dalton. They even reported the direction he was heading and what kind of horse he was riding.

Towerly did not appear to have any interest in hiding out. He went to his father's house. This was the first place the deputies looked for him.

True to form, Towerly did not try to escape, but reacted just as Smith had done, and came out shooting. This time, he killed E. A. Stokley, another Deputy.

Towerly had seen how this approach turned out for Smith. Though Deputy Stokley fell, the other deputies that accompanied him returned fire, striking Towerly eight times.

Though he was wounded and, on the ground, Towerly refused to surrender. He called for his father to bring him another gun so he could keep fighting.

The congressional report on the incident attributes the death of Towerly to Deputy Bill Moody.

Being a Deputy Marshal in the Indian Territory continued to be an astonishingly deadly job. Deputy Moody too was shot in the line of duty–killed in March of 1889.

Moody met his end attempting an arrest that, on the surface at least, seems eerily similar to his pursuit of Towerly and the death of his partner, Deputy Stokley.

Moody was chasing Jeff Berryhill, a murderer that Moody believed had chosen to hole up in the home of his parents.

With the attempt on Towerly, the deputies had moved cautiously on foot, but were still spotted. The very first shot fired from the house killed Moody's partner–Deputy Stokley.

This time, though, Moody had a different plan. Caution be damned. Moody's new plan was to full-out charge the house on horseback. Moody and his partner galloped toward the house.

Just as stealth had failed him previously, this new attack strategy was equally problematic. Deputy Moody was shot by a man named William Brunner who was inside the house.

Brunner wasn't who Moody was after, but when he saw the men on horseback riding at the house, he didn't have time to inquire about their intentions. Instead, he shot Moody—a shot that proved fatal.

There's a chance that Moody's death could have been avoided by a simple announcement of the deputies' intentions. After the shooting began, and Moody fell, the other deputy (likely panicked, as he, too, had been shot) called out and told the shooters they were lawmen.

As unlikely as it seems, the announcement worked. Brunner put down his guns. Despite his tactical advantage, he and the others inside the house surrendered.

Brunner later claimed he fired out of a sense of self preservation, as he thought he was under attack.

Moody had not identified himself as a lawman, so Brunner was convicted of manslaughter, in this case, and not murder.

All of this, sadly, was based on the misinformation that Jeff Berryhill—the original man they were hunting—was in the house. He wasn't. His brother William, oddly enough, was also wanted for murder, but he never fired a shot.

William Berryhill was taken into Judge Parker's court, where he was tried and acquitted.

As for Moody's partner in the Brunner debacle—we come full circle. The man that called out and announced he was a deputy was Grat Dalton. The Grat Dalton who was deputy Frank Dalton's younger brother. The Grat Dalton that, not long after, would be killed on the other side of the law.

Grat had received a real education about the life of a deputy. His brother was killed serving as a deputy and now he witnessed his partner gunned down as well. Grat had taken a bullet in the arm charging the house with Moody. It must have been a tough couple of years.

You can never say for sure exactly what effect the botched arrest attempt had on Grat or his other brothers, but you could assume it did not make law enforcement seem like the ideal career choice.

Was all of this violence worth it? Frank Dalton died making what should have been a routine arrest. Ultimately six people, including two deputies, died.

The one Dalton bother that lived long enough to record his thoughts was Emmett. He in fact wrote two books—*Beyond the Law* and *When the Daltons Rode*—both were made into movies. Emmett's books are not noted for their accuracy but are interesting none the less.

Emmett Dalton's take on the Deputy Moody shooting is that Brunner thought he was coming under fire by a rival faction of Creeks. That was the basis of Brunner's claim of self-defense.

Emmett wasn't there when Moody was killed, but his horse was. Moody, as Emmett tells it, had borrowed Emmett's horse for the arrest attempt. Emmett blames Moody's fatal charge at the house on the skittish horse, and not Moody. The horse, Emmett suggests, bolted and Moody had no choice but to go along.

Who knows? It is a strange story, but his brother was there—so the story could be sound.

When Emmett retells the story of his brother Frank's killer Towerly, it too takes a fanciful twist.

One particular embellishment centered around Towerly's parents—a homespun couple presented as an idealized version of attentive and loving family. It is hard to see how Emmett could have known the true nature of this clan, but he cooked up some loving dialogue between them just before Will Towerly was killed.

Again, I'm questioning motives—but Emmett may have wanted to give the impression that all outlaws, no matter how notorious, had mothers that loved them.

In Emmett's version, the doting mother is attentively making food for her son before he hits the trail. A more common depiction of the Towerly bunch shows them wrestling Deputy Moody into their house in an attempt to keep him from shooting young Towerly. The wrestlers included Will's sister and his mother. These women were tough.

The Towerly women were not the only women involved in all of this shooting.

Remember, just after Frank Dalton was shot, Mrs. Dixon ran out to attend to Dave Smith. Cole testified that Mrs. Dixon grabbed Smith's gun, which is why Cole shot her. Was Cole just trying to justify his actions, or was she about to join the fray?

Lizzie Smith in turn testified that she grabbed Cole's gun before the shooting started when he first approached the tent. It did not appear that well-armed deputies struck fear into the hearts of Indian Territory women.

End notes...

A bunch of the people in this book all ended up in the Oak Cemetery in Fort Smith, Arkansas. Deputy Cole is there as well as Elias Boudinot. Near them is the Payne family plot which includes the brothers, who I believe, owned "Payne's

Clearing" where Deputy Dalton was killed. They lived well into the twentieth century and were remembered well on this side of the river making the local papers for golf tournaments. Gabriel's obituary credits him with establishing the road system for Sequoyah County Oklahoma. As prominent as Houston and Gabriel were in Sequoyah County, they seemed to have disappeared from that history. It may be that they were more citizens of Fort Smith than Oklahoma. They did have a long-standing presence on both sides of the river. Another possibility is due to their Cherokee connections that they were marginalized when the whites became the dominate culture. We will likely never know.

Sources include: *Tragedy Stops* by Darrell M. Hull Oklahombres Winter 1996

Deadly Affrays by Robert Ernst

Congressional Record Vol. 19 page 4822, 1888

When the Daltons Rode by Emmett Dalton

Investigation before Commissioner Brizzolara 1887, Fort Smith National Historic Site files

* * *

Sometimes you find these odd threads that run through a story in unexpected ways. Take Trent Thompson for instance. This fine young man, I am proud to say, is my nephew, and this project began with Trent.

My first introduction to Frank Dalton was on a little folded piece of cardboard that had the names of all the deputies killed in the line of duty in the Indian territory. The historic site in Fort Smith decided something more was needed. My nephew Trent had taken this as his Eagle Scout project. His project was making some fifty substantial wooden markers.

When the committee to select the site for the US Marshal Museum came to town, these markers were the final tribute presented to them. When the head of the Marshal service made the announcement that we were to be the official site he also announced that young Trent Thompson was named the Citizen of the Year for the US Marshal Service. He and his family were flown to Washington to receive the award.

The museum's building is now complete, as well as the Hall of Honor for fallen deputies, Frank's name is now on that wall. I think you can follow the tread so far, but it continues.

Trent is now married, and it is his wife that teaches in the Moffett school. She was the one that told me about their outstanding reading program. There is one final twist in the thread. The young man that testifies in the Cole ferry shooting, is an ancestor of Trent's through his father's family.

Notes on why this matters today

There is a lot of violence in this story. Dalton was killed. Deputies were killed. Many innocent people, too—killed.

We are still living in violent times as I write this. Seems there is a mass shooting every week.

As the case of Ned Christie, more than a century ago, illustrates, law enforcement can be problematic. I'd like to believe that we would have figured out these conundrums. We've had plenty of time. Yet we continue to face lingering questions about the role of law enforcement in our society. More than a century later we are still debating how to define the good guys, and the bad.

Even more perplexing is something deeply rooted in the American psyche. Literate Americans in 1887 were hooked on dime-store novelizations of outlaws and villainy. Fictitious exaggerations of people like Billy the Kid exploded in pop culture even while the historical figures themselves were still making actual history, and this rebellious spirit captivated the staid and complacent and polite.

Nothing has changed. Humans still seem to celebrate evil over good. This little slice of history seems to illustrate this well.

The "Dalton Gang" spawned numerous books, and movies. This is the first one I am aware of about the good Dalton.

Maybe we value the little man's struggle against power. The Gang took on the monolithic and faceless railroads. They knocked over banks. A normal twenty-eight-year-old man risking his life every day, to support his mother and family, and at the same time attempting to bring some order to the chaos…? Maybe that is not as interesting, but it still deserves remembering.

That's the first reason you have this book.

There is also the contrast between Frank Dalton, and James Cole. Dalton strikes me as a decent sort, going forth to do his duty. Cole not as much.

Are we not—still—trying to find a way to attract the right kind of law enforcement officers, and assure that they survive in these troubled times?

This is a question we have been asking since the wild west, and likely long before that.

Another lesson I personally take from writing this, is the value of cooperation. My contributor and I likely do not agree on many issues. So, what? Does that mean that we must see each other as "Evil"?

Because we disagree on some things, does that should mean we cannot work together? I don't buy it, at all. We came to the task, finding common ground, and produced a book. For me that is something.

There is one final important lesson in this book—another key element that transcends the chasm of time between 1887 and now. Dave Smith told at least two people he intended to shoot someone. No one seems to have reported this. A lot of killing resulted. It clearly would have taken much more effort in 1887 to make a report.

It is amazingly easy now, yet it still does not happen often enough.

Lives are at stake. Denial is still raging in full force. Someone usually knows that there is a dangerous individual out there, but no one takes action. Please take them seriously, this is literally life and death, it always has been, and tragically still is.

We can work together, all of us doing our part, on whatever political side, and help stop this waste of life. A lot of this is that simple.

In the middle of the night again – November 26, 2022

Tomorrow is the 135th anniversary of Frank Dalton's killing.

I think I should go to where Frank died. I called up, well… *texted*, Dave the contributor and said let's try to get the picture of the house. I mean there is a house that was there and still is there on the land where it all happened. A Payne house from "Payne's Clearing". We do not have a picture of it.

The book is finished and we ain't got no picture. Really? It seems to be a huge missing piece don't you think? It is not for lack of effort, but how far do you go?

Across the river I am an outsider, an intruder, a borderline stalker! The house was purchased from the Payne Family in the 1930's by the Hawkins family. Mrs. Hawkins has been quite supportive and generous with her knowledge of the property. She put me in touch with the Payne family. I am clear that I have her permission to include the house in this book. She does not live in the house she lives on this side of the river in Fort Smith. Lived—God rest her soul; she died about a month ago.

The lady that does live there has a deep love for the house and the surrounding area, of that I have no doubt. She has generously spoken with me on a number of occasions. I referred to her in a previous chapter as one of the sources that I had high hopes for. For whatever reason I have never been in the house or seen any documentation from the occupant. Please understand it is her home, I am the intruder.

When I contacted Dave about getting the picture, he said should we contact them first. Who knows? The last time I asked permission I was given a "not now" answer. Technically I understand I do not have to have the occupant's permission. It sure would be better to have it. I would feel better anyway.

But there's one more Payne's Clearing-Moffett quagmire.

At this writing all of Moffett's future looks bleak. The river may finally win its long struggle with the little town. FEMA is putting the place on probation. Without the FEMA flood protection, it is hard to see how the community will survive. If the community cannot fix the flood issue in the next year, they are all on their own. The few that are still there have more to worry about than my little book.

The shining light of Moffett is the school. There is hope that it will find a way to survive.

Appendix

The following are trial transcripts from the period of this book. Most relate directly to the historical figures we've discussed and the killing of Frank Dalton.

In our attempt to transcribe these hand-written documents, we've left in the peculiar and often stilted syntax of the original documentation of the spoken testimonies. Paragraph breaks are maintained in alignment with the hand-written notation. All of these files are housed in the collections of Fort Smith's National Historic Park.

United States versus Leander Dixon and Joseph Pierson for murder.

United States of America
Western District of Arkansas
Before Brizzolara, United States Commissioner

On the 29th day of November 1887, came the United States of America, the Plaintiff in this cause, WM. H. Clayton, Esq., U.S Attorney, and the defendants in their own proper persons, in custody of the Marshal and by their Attorneys Mess. Edemensten and Geo. W. Grace when the following testimony was heard and proceedings had, to-wit:

J.R. Cole duly sworn says:

I reside at Fort Smith Ark. Frank Dalton is dead. He was a deputy US marshal for this district, he had a writ for a man by the name of Dave Smith for Larceny and I had a writ also for him for introducing and selling whiskey. Saturday evening last I understand that Smith was up here at Payne's Clearing near the Cook Lease about four miles from the city. I went over to where Dep Dalton was camped on the other side of the river about a mile from here. Found Dalton at his camp, got to his camp Saturday evening late about five o'clock. Dalton told me after I told him what I was after to get down and stay all night, that he knew him when he seen him and that he could go after him with me in the morning and get him Sunday Morning. We got up got our breakfast and went to where we understood Smith was camped at that was in

Payne's Clearing near Cook Place. When we got to where we could see the tent we rode over to it. Dalton got down from his horse on south side of tent and I got down on North side of tent. When we rode up to tent did not see any body. The first thing I heard was Dalton saying "Hold up! Hold Up we do not want any trouble, we did not come here for any trouble". He said hold up three or four times. When I heard this I ran around to front of tent and saw a man with his back towards me said to have been Smith facing Dalton he fired and Dalton said "Oh! Lord I am killed", then I shot the man that shot Dalton/ I tried to shoot him right in the back, did not see with what kind of a weapon he (smith) fired with. When Smith shot, Smith fired across the South west corner of tent. When he fired I was at north west corner of tent. When Smith fired I fired and Smith fell. At the same instance a woman ran out of tent and looked like she was coming to catch hold of me and a man come right up behind her firing right over her shoulder at me. As I went to shoot him, she caught my gun and threw it up and I fired up in the air. I struck my foot against something and fell backwards. As I got up the woman had disappeared and this fellow shot me. The man that shot me is this man Dixon who is in now wounded and in jail. He shot me in the breast he grazed my breast a little. At the same time I fired and I think I hit him. Then this man whirled around about twice and went into the tent. Then some one fired at me from the tent. I then ran behind a tree and parties from the tent still continued shooting at me. There seemed to have been two shooting at me from the tent. At the last shot I fired some man and a woman left the tent and made for the brush. After I left and had gone about two hundred yards two shots were fired. I did not see Defd Pierson at all there were two parties in the tent I never seen. The woman that caught my gun I understand her name to be Mrs. Smith the wife of Smith that was killed. Do not know who the man or woman were that made for the brush. We got to tent at about nine o'clock Sunday morning. The first person I saw was Smith coming from tent and Dalton backing off telling him to hold up that he wanted no trouble. When Dalton was shot he kind of doubled up and backed out to the back of tent where he fell. I paid no further attention to Dalton as the firing commenced to be very rapid. This was in Cherokee Nation. Dixon shot three over the woman's shoulder and the third shot hit me. The women were screaming and the shooting was so fast that if anything was said I did not hear it. There seemed to be three or four women there. Dixon said nothing while firing at me nor I to him. I was shooting at him with a Winchester. Dalton has a Winchester in his hands and a six shooter around him. Dalton fired no shots. Smith was killed. I understood he died shortly after he was shot. As I ran from the tent to a tree and passed by Dalton and I asked him if he was killed and he never spoke nor moved. I stayed by the tree a little bit and I spoke to him there and he never spoke and when I left I lift him for dead. His gun was lying on the ground at his feet. I was at the time and I am now a Deputy US Marshal for this district. Never seen anyone come up. But seen other parties about 150 or 200 yards from the tent. There was an old man at a tent south of this tent and I called to him to help get Dalton away. I think there was one other there besides the tent at which the difficulty occurred. This tent was about 150 yards from where difficulty occurred. No body came near while I was there. I am a white man.

James Raley:

I know Deft Pierson when I see him. Know Dixon when I see him. Have been working with them in clearing on Payne Place for the last two weeks. Knew tent where difficulty occurred at I was also camping in a tent about 100 yards from this tent. This tent where difficulty occurred was put up by defendant. Deft were occupying the tent. There were three women and these two defendants. The women were Dixon's wife and Pierson's wife and Smith's wife. I seen they were also in the tent there were none outside when Marshals rode up. Smith had come there on Wednesday night and remained there I could see him every day there in passing about. On Sunday morning I was standing in front of my tent when I seen two men come riding up. I supposed them to be Marshals from the way were armed. They rode by pretty close to the tent and dismounted one ran up to the mouth of tent and the other went on behind the tent. The one that went to the mouth of the tent sort of poked his gun into mouth of tent looked in and gave back then and by this time Smith came out of tent as the man gave back and fired. Smith was at the door of the tent shooting across the tent the way this man gave back. I supposed he was shooting at the man. When Smith fired Dalton came around to the end of the tent and was shot there or fell there. When Smith fired there was another shot fired from inside of the tent out at the south west corner of tent. You could hardly distinguish between the two shoots. But Smiths shot was the first shot. Dalton fell as soon as the shot from the tent was made. Then the next shot fired outside of the tent killed Smith he fell, I suppose Deputy Cole shot him. There was after this some more shooting but I could not tell if it was in the tent or behind the tent. Directly Smith was shot, Mrs. Dixon, Mrs. Smith and Mrs. Pierson came out of tent and Mrs. Pierson kept on running. When Mrs. Pierson come out of there Deft Pierson come out also and they ran off together. When Mrs. Dixon come out she sort of stooped down to where Smith was and she was shot and she fell. Mrs. Smith stood there. The first I seen of Dixon he came out and picked up his wife and tried to help her up and he was shot. That is all

I know about that. I seen Dixon come out of tent. I could not see Cole from where I was standing. I did not see Dixon fire any. Do not know who killed the woman. There was another man come there with Smith when he came never heard his name. I seen him fire at Dalton after he was down. He came out of the tent he was the last one that came out of then and went around then to within four or five feet of where Dalton was lying and took deliberate aim at Dalton and shot him in the head with a Winchester. He shot at him twice and stayed there two or three minutes and went off a foot. He went out north. Dixon has sort of stooped down and was picking his wife up when he was shot. I do not know if Dixon had fired any shots at all at any time. I know he fired no shots after he came out of tent, I never seen the man that came with Smith until they were all shot down. Mrs. Smith stayed there where Smith has fallen all throughout the difficulty. There was a fire outside of the tent. Smith fell between them and fire right at corner of tent. Mrs. Dixson fell right by Smith. Dixon fell by her. I heard nothing except the women screaming. All the firing that I heard from the tent was this fellow that ran off behind the tent shooting at Mr. Cole. Except the pistol shot from tent at the time Smith fired. There must have been either or ten shots fired around there altogether. Did not hear Cole call me. After it was all over I went up there. I found Smith shot and Mrs. and Mr. Dixon also shot and Dalton none of them were dead but the deputy Marshal. Cannot tell where about in the body Dalton was shot. But know he was shot in the head by the fellow that ran off. Smith was shot about his left shoulder I believe. Do not know where Mrs. Dixon was shot at. I heard Smith talking to his wife but could not understand them. Smith died at about ten o'clock that morning. Mrs. Dixon lived about five minutes after I got there. After I got there Deft Pierson and his wife came up I did not hear him say anything when he came back nor when I seen him running off. Mrs. Dixon was taken down to the house of Mrs. Lindale and laid out. Smith was buried last night. Pierson went after Mrs. Dixon's folks and they came and got her and took her home. Mrs. Pierson stayed until we all got them fixed away. When Smith died they took him to an out house. And when they took Dixon off they moved their things to that out house. Mrs. Lindale, Bryant and Geo Conner seen this difficulty they were as near to it as I was. They were at their own house a little way from my tent.

The cause is continued to Nov 30/1887

James Raley recalled:

Deft Pierson came out from tent directly after the firing commenced, never spoke to Pierson about the matter.

James Fletcher:

Know Smith well, acquainted with him. Do not know Dep Dalton nor defendants. Never seen Deft Dixon until Saturday last. Dixon and Smith lived in this tent. I suppose Pierson lived there too. On Saturday I went to mill in returning from mill I met Smith and Towerly this man that ran off. Dave Smith turned around and said to me "I am going to kill Marshal Cole before Monday night". Towerly never spread his lips. Smith turned around and rode off with Turner ahead of me. I was in wagon my mother and Frank Gibson were with me in wagon. Met Smith in road right by Gabe Payne's house this was about sun set. Smith and Towerly went off in a gallop and left us. Smith has a Winchester swinging on his saddle. Towerly has his six-shooter buckled around him and pulled right in front of him. I live half a mile from were difficulty accrued. About on house after the difficulty went over to tent when I got there Dixon was lying down by fire outside and Smith was lying in tent Mrs. Dixon had been carried to Woodall's house. Pierson had gone to town so I was told. Never spoke to Pierson about it. The first time I seen Pierson was here on yesterday. Smith said something to his wife for her to do something but could not hear what it was as there were so many between where I was and Smith.

Lizzy Smith:

David Smith was my husband. Dixon and his wife and Pierson and his wife lived at this tent. I was there on a visit. Dixon is my brother. Pierson is no relative of mine. Pierson's wife is Mr. Dixon's sister. On Weds day night prior to the shooting my husband came to the tent. It was after dark a little while. Willie Towerly was with him. They came a horseback. This was the first time I had ever seen Towerly. They stayed there all the time and never left until Saturday morning when Dave saddled his horse and went off and returned in about ten minutes. Then when Dave comeback Towerly got on the horse Smith was riding and left and was gone about half an hour He went out though the bottoms. They were just riding around. We, Mr. and Mrs. Dixon, Mr. and Mrs. Pierson Towerly my husband and I were setting down in tent eating our breakfast. I got up and went to get some bread and I saw Mr. Cole come running with a Winchester. I said "Lord a mercy, yonder comes a man with a Winchester" and I just whirled back and he was there with his gun jabbed inside of tent. I jerked his gun to one side and said don't do that. The way the gun went it looked like it was towards the table. I jumped at the gun again he having shoved me back. I never got hold of gun the second time. I was right nearby between my husband and Cole. When I jumped again Dave Smith the first I seen of him had his gun (Winchester) presented at Cole and they both fired about the same time. When I jumped for gun Cole gave back the least little bit. My husband made about two steps and got outside of tent Cole never came in tent. When Smith fired Cole he ran and he got and he got out of my sight. They were facing one another right close when Smith fired. The whole front of tent was open. When Smith fired Cole was kind of around the corner of tent but very little. They both fired about together. When Cole ran somebody shot Smith in the Back and he fell I guess Dalton killed him. When Cole ran he had made two steps towards Cole with his Winchester in his hands when he was shot. When Smith and Cole fired I was standing outside of corner of tent nearly between them. My hair in front was burned by the firing. They did not tell anybody to give up, if they had they would have surrendered I suppose then to have died. When Dave fell Mrs. Dixon ran out of tent and grabbed me and hollowed as mercy they have killed Dave. And Mr. Cole shot her. Cole ran behind a tree and I seen him a shooting and I saw the smoke of his guns. And she hollowed of lord I am killed then Mr. Dixon jumped out of the tent and stooped over her and started to pull her up and as he had his head stooped over her he was shot. Mr. Cole shot him from behind a tree. About the time Dixon was shot Mr. Pierson and his wife came running out of tent and ran down towards fence there. Then Towerly left the tent and went out behind the tent and I heard two shots and I suppose that is where he killed Dalton. I hears Dalton out there praying to Towerly not to kill him. When Dalton shot Smith I do not know what became of Dalton. There were shots fired from inside of the tent. Just as Smith was shot and fell fired commenced from tent. There did not seem to be but one person firing from tent. I know there was but one shooting from tent as there was only one six shooter to be shot. The only arms inside of tent was one six shooter but Willie Towerly had it on. The Winchester belonged to Dave. Dixon nor Pierson had no arms. I guess Towerly was shooting at Cole when Cole was shooting. He was shooting from back of tent. As soon as Dalton shot Smith I did not see him any more. I was standing all the time right there over have until it was all over. I guess Cole shot some seven or eight times. I guess Dave did not shoot over three or four shots. I do not think Dalton fired by the one shot that killed Dave. I guess Towerly emptied his pistol. Towerly came out of tent and picked up Dave's Winchester and shot Dalton with it. Walking around to back of tent. When Towerly walked up to Dalton. Dalton was lying down on ground by a stump back of the tent. I looked through a crack in tent and seen him. I heard Dalton say to Towerly that he was not ready to die. Please don't kill me. Towerly never answered but shot him twice. This was about nine o'clock last Sunday morning. I suppose Smith knew Cole but not Dalton. I do not know whether or not he knew Cole. He said after he was shot that if Marshal Cole had told him to surrender he would have surrendered. After the difficulty they first I seen of Pierson he was helping to take Mrs. Dixon to a house. Towerly left a foot he took a bridle. Dave's horse is gone. He took the Winchester and pistol. Towerly looks to be about nineteen or twenty years. Towerly's father lives at Stringtown. Dave fired at Cole all the shots he fired. He fired three or four shots he fired. He fired three or four shots at him before Dalton shot Smith. Dave after he was shot never fired any more. Dave fired all his shots standing right there in front of tent. Mr. Johnson was the first person that come up to us after the difficulty Johnson has gone off with this man Roger to Webbers Falls. Dixon I think was shot in back below neck. Dave was shot in back sort of between his shoulders. I came there at this tent with Dixon and Pierson.

Cross:

The only arms in tent were a Winchester and a six shooter belonging to Dave. When I grabbed gun of Coles and threw it to one side the gun fired in then. I went nearly to the fire with Cole when I tried to grab Cole's gun again the second time. All this time I do not know what Dave was doing. Do not think any shot fired from tent until after Smith fell. When Dave fell I was standing close to him. When she (Mrs. Dixon) said Lord A Mercy in a minute after she came up to me she was shot. The shot that killed her came from behind tree where Cole was firing from. Dixon when he came from tent had no arms. When his wife fell Dixon was just inside of tent close to me and he came running out when his wife fell. Dixon fired no shots having nothing to shoot with. After the shooting I turned Dave over he was lying on his face. I asked him if he was killed he said yes that he was going to die he was killed. Then he said I wished to God Marshal Cole had said for me to surrender I would have give up. Then after he spoke of getting well he lived for two or three hours after the difficulty.

Re-Direct:

We had just moved down from Ronteses house to tent. Ronteses house was about as far from here to courthouse from then. Cole was at front of tent of course as he could not have jabbed his gun in tent. Did not see Dalton shoot Dave.

James Bryan:

Know Defts. Never seen Smith until that morning. Never seen Towerly only at a distance. I seen difficulty. I was standing in my yard at the time. About two or three shot fired just as I stepped out of my house at the south side. As I got to corner of house where I could see I seen Cole leave the mouth on front of tent and went down towards fence east of tent. And he went about twenty or thirty yards from tent and he turned and fired as there was a shot fired from tent at him from mouth of tent right over the corner of tent and Cole got behind a tree. I seen the man but could not say who fired it. As I was not close enough to see. When Cole got behind tree he loaded his gun and stepped backwards and fried another shot he went back again and loaded and fired from tree two shoots and he advanced back some eight or ten steps to another tree and he fired one shot there and worked there at his gun some little length of time. Then he left and got in road. Then Towerly come out from tent and fired at Cole when Cole was about 20 steps from three. Towerly fired at him with a Winchester. As he came out of tent he picked up the Winchester at the mouth of the tent. After Towerly shot at Cole he came around then and shot Dalton. He shot at Dalton there. I never did see Smith until after the shooting was over. I seen two men fall. I supposed they were Dixon and Smith. Dixon had just raised up at mouth of tent when he fell. Smith was the one that is said to have fired at Cole or rather that I seen fire at Cole. He fired across tent as soon as Cole fired back at him why he fell. Dixon fell the last one. Dixon fell at the first shot Cole made from the tree. Cole was sort of back end of tent behind tree. When Cole was shooting there was someone at back end of tent shooting at Cole all the time. I did not see Marshals when they rode up. I seen Cole the first time just as he whirled from mouth of tent on south side of tent. Dalton the first I seen of him was coming from north side of tent to back end and fell at north east corner of then neat stump and crawled up to the stump and got behind it. He staid there until there until this Kid come out. When the Kid come out he picked up Daltons gun right at the front of the tent and put a cartridge in it and went half way of tent and fired at Mr. Cole. He then re-loaded it and went to where Dalton was behind the stump and he shot at him and just before the smoke of the gun he (Dalton) threw up his hand his right hand and said something to him but I could hear what he said and then the kid shot and the man fell over at the crack of the gun. Then he re-loaded his gun and starched it out as if he was close to him and came still closer then the first shot he made and fired again. He then turned and went back the same way he came and placed gun against the wall of tent and he went inside and he came out with another Winchester in his hands and he picked up a bridle and blanket with his left hand he had gun in right hand and went off down a ridge and this is the last I seen of him. When I first seen Dalton he was on the ground crawling on his all fours towards stump when I seen Dalton Cole had exchanged the first shot and was making towards that tree. After the two or three first shots and as Mr. Cole whirled to run I seen Deft Pierson. He came out the front of tent with his baby in his arms and jumped across the fence they had built in front and he went about ten or twenty feet from fence and he stopped until his wife came to him and he went in front of his wife and she after him and they went about 100 yards when the shooting was all over and he turned to come back and Pierson took hold of his sister (Mrs. Dixon) and I supposed turned her and took her out of the mud and then came to me. Mrs. Pierson remained by Mrs. Dixon. Deft Pierson got me to carry Mrs. Dixon to a house but mine was small and crowded and we took her to my brother-in-law Mr. C.L. Woodall. A man by the name of Johnson got there to then the first one. Deft Pierson called to Johnson that his sister was dead. That they had killed his sister and Johnson come on up to tent in a run. Pierson came to me. Never seen anything of Mrs. Dixon until after the difficulty when I went to tent. Never seen anything of Mrs. Smith until after I went up there after the difficulty was over. Mrs. Dixon had two children. One was about two years old and the one between six or nine months old. The oldest a gild and the youngest a boy. Mrs. Smith had one child six or eight months old. Mrs. Pierson has one child about six or eight months old. Of the three shots fired as I come out of house two shots were fired as close together that you could hardly distinguish them as I stepped on to the ground. There was a little difference in third shot. The two first was one a little one and one a big one. All three shots was close together. As I turned around corner of my house was when I could see that tent. The tent is built three logs high with cloth stretched over the top of it. I seen two Winchesters the one Towerly took off and the one lying up against the tent when I got there. Seen a pistol lying at stump when Dalton was lying at right up against the stump between two roots. I took it to be Dalton's pistol. Towerly handled two Winchester during the shooting he got first gun on the front of tent he came out and picked it up. Smith fell near south west corner of tent with his head right towards my house. The same Winchester that he first picked up Towerly placed it against corner of tent and came out with another Winchester in his hand. The Winchester that he picked up at corner of tent belonged to Dalton. The one Towerly came out of the tent belonged to Smith. Smith was laying partly across Mrs. Dixon feet and part of her dress. Everything indicated that Mrs. Dixon was the first person shot. But cannot say when and how she was shot as I did not see her until after the difficulty. When I seen Mrs. Smith she was by Mr. Smith sitting there holding him up her baby was carried to my house after the shooting three babies were carried to my house Mrs. Pierson still carried her baby, I examined Mrs. Dixon's wounds. Mrs. Dixon was wounded in her left breast right below her breast. From the size of hole I think it was a Winchester wound. Smith begged his wife not to tell anything that took place first yet that he thought he would get well. Never heard him say anything more until he was almost dying when he said by God I guess Mr. Cole got a pretty good wad as well as myself. Raley and Johnson were present when I heard Smith begging his wife not to tell anything that occurred when I first went up. Never had any conversation with Dixon and Pierson about it. He also said in first conversation that if Cole had come to him and asked him to surrender he would have done so before there was any shooting done. Smith said he know Cole. Smith never said anything about Dalton. On yesterday morning as we were coming here I asked Mrs. Smith what Mr. Smith meant when he begged her not to tell anything that took place first. She said it was concerning the shooting that he thought he could get well and if he got well that he thought it would go harder with him if he shot and he did not want her to tell that he shot. I was about 100 or 120 yards from shooting. Mrs. Raley had gone out before I had Raley is my father-in-law. Cole has a Winchester.

I. L. Windall:

Know Defts: Never seen Smith until Tuesday a week ago: Towery was with him: Seen them when they came to Mr. Raleys camp inquiring for Dixon and Pierson: Raley told him where their tent was: Seen them every night and morning after this: Seen them on Saturday at Mr Bells gin: That is I seen Towery: Smith was at home on Saturday morning: They went armed Smith had a Winchester and Towerly a six shooter: Had seen them on Sunday morning knocking around camp: Smith had come after water 20 minutes before the difficulty: He had his Winchester never seen him any other way only armed: Never spoke to either of these men before the difficulty: I was standing in the door when I seen Cole and Dalton ride in side by side until they got within 30 feet of tent when they drew out their Winchester: Got off their horses and turned them loose and one went (Mr. Cole) on north side of tent. Dalton went to front of tent with his Winchester up in both hands he was before the tent: He did not have Winchester thrust in the tent: he jumped back from front of tent Smith came out and as Dalton got around corner of tent Smith fired across corner of tent and shot Dalton Smith shot him with his Winchester: When Smith fired on Dalton Cole was behind Smith at the other corner of tent shot Smith: Dalton when shot fell right at back end of tent and Cole left tent and fell back behind a tree: Then the next shooting was from corner of tent inside of tent shooting at Mr. Cole: After that shooting was over: I seen Towery come out of tent with Winchester in his hands go where Dalton was laying: He (Dalton) got up his arms sort of on his all fours and asked him for God sake not to shoot him anymore that he was a dead man then: Then Towerly shot Dalton twice: he had gun aimed at him: The first shot Towerly fired at him he was about five or six feet from him and he took two steps more towards him aimed at him and shot him a second time: Towerly came back in tent came out picked up a bridle and blanket and a Winchester and left: he went down below house a peace and caught one of Smith's horses and rode off: Smith fired first shot: I never seen Dixon at all until after the difficulty: I did not see Mrs. Dixon nor Mrs. Smith until after the difficulty Deft Pierson came out of tent at the time the two first shots were fired with his baby in his arms and ran about 20 steps and staid there until his wife came out to him and they ran about a hundred yards and stopped and they staid there until difficulty was over and then him and three other men brought his sister Mrs. Dixon to my house: There must have been about 20 shoots fired in all.

George Conner:

I know none of the men. I went to Mr. Bryan's to play with his boy and I heard 2 shots and I went to the door. I seen around the house before I could see the tent. When I got around the house I seen Mr. Cole running to a tree and shoot twice from the tree. There was some fellow inside of the tent shooting at Cole from the corner of the tent. When this shooting was going on I seen Pearson run off from the tent, his wife with him with baby in her arms and run down in clearing somewheres. Mrs. Dixon was shot after Mr. Pierson come out, she was shot right at the mouth of the tent, I could not tell you who shot her. I did not see her fall at all. I did not see her when she was shot. I do not know when she was shot. I am about 15 years old. Mr. Cole was back of a tree behind the tent. Seen Mrs. Smith at the mouth of tent when shooting was going on. I did not see Mrs. Dixon when she fell. Smith, when I went out, was at the mouth of the tent shooting at Mr. Dalton. Dalton was behind tent laying down behind a stump. Dalton was not shooting at Smith. I seen Smith when he fell. Cole shot Smith from behind the tree. Smith was shot in the back. Smith was in front of Dalton behind a stump back of tent. Cole was behind Dalton behind a tree and sort of to the right of Mr. Dalton.

Whereupon the further examination of this cause is continued to Dec 87.

George Conner recalled:

When we heard shots, Mr. Bryan and I were standing in the door. Could not tell you how many shots were fired when we stepped around house, so that we could see the tent. When I got around so that I could see, Mr. Cole was running to get behind tree, if he shot while he was a running I did not see it. Smith was standing at mouth of tent shooting at Dalton. Dalton was behind tent lying behind stump. Did not see Dalton shoot any. When I went up to him after the difficulty I seen a pistol lying near his arms. He was lying on his side when I went up to him. After the difficulty I only went up to where Dalton was, saw him then I left going home. I see them lying there but paid no attention to them. I never seen Mrs. Smith at all. I seen Mr. Smith when he fell. He fell at the mouth of the tent. Cole shot him. When Smith fell Cole was shooting from behind the tree. Smith was shooting at Dalton when Cole shot Smith. Cole left the tree after he shot Smith. I seen Cole when he shot Dixon. Dixon had stooped down to pick up his wife, and I didn't know how Cole came to shoot him, nor what part of Dixon's person became exposed as he stood up in the act of picking up his wife. I did not see any of the other children at all except Pearson's baby. Never seen Towerly at all until he ran out of the tent and shot Dalton. He ran out and picked up the gun that was lying at the corner of the tent belonging to Dalton, went up to him and shot him. When Towerly went up to Dalton to shot him Dalton threw up his hands but I could not hear what Dalton said, Towerly shot at him twice.

Cross Examination:

I did not see Dixon have anything in his hands. After Dixon was shot Towerly ran out of the tent and shot Dalton. As soon as Dixon was shot Cole ran away from the tree. Cole, from where he was, could see Dixon stooping to pick up his wife.

Re-Direct:

The corner of the tent is not the mouth of the tent. I never seen Mrs. Dixon fall at all. I seen Mr. Dixon fall. I seen Dixon run out of the tent and pick up his wife. Dixon ran out there after Mr. Smith fell. I could not tell you how many shots were fired from the time Dixon ran out to pick up his wife until he fell.

James Bryan recall says:

I noticed last night 3 shots that were in his clothes. There were 2 shots both in back. They were just an inch and a half apart. One seemed from the size of the holes, to be a pistol and the other a Winchester. His clothes were not powder burnt. Mrs. Smith's clothes where shot, one ball passed through her clothes between her legs and the front of her dress had some 3 or 4 holes. Smith fell at the shot fired by Cole as Cole was running to the tree. Smith had fired at Cole before he, Cole, fired at him. I do not know who shot Dalton. I did not see shot that caused Dalton to fall. There was shooting going on from inside of the tent all the time. This was from the southeast corner of the tent. After Smith fell the next shot of Cole's killed Dixon. While Cole was firing when Dixon came from the tent Dixon's head and shoulders became exposed and he was hit by a bullet.

James Raley recalled says:

Cole went to the mouth of the tent when he did so he kind of looked in. His gun never fired. Smith fired the first shot. There was not shot fired until Smith fired in the direction of Mr. Cole. Just as Smith fired Dalton came around the end of the tent. And about the time that Smith fired there was a gun or pistol fired from inside of the tent, at the southeast corner of the tent and Dalton fell. The shot that killed Smith, the gunshot that killed Smith, the gun came from the direction of where Mr. Cole was. I heard no conversion of any kind between Mr. and Mrs. Smith after the difficulty.

James Fletcher recalled says:

I seen Smith and Towerly before they had any conversion with me. I was coming in a wagon to the river from my folks and they passed me on the road and came on towards the river and I stopped on the bank by Payne's. They came back from the river, this was about six or five o'clock last Saturday evening. A colored man named Sam Thurman was standing there at the bank of the river as Smith was talking to me. Towerly never opened his mouth. Smith was riding a sort of sorrel horse and Towerly was riding a deep bay horse with both ears split, with white feet clear up to the knees.

Cross:

Smith knew me. Smith said "How are you, Fletcher?" I had not seen Smith for some years before this. He then asked me if I had seen Cole pass. I told him he had done passed and had gone to the river. He said he was going on and follow him and if he could get site of him he would kill him before Monday night. Cole had passed me about half and hour before this coming to town. Cole had been out summonsing witnesses in Bell Fletchers case.

Cause continued to Jan 88

January 7 A.D. 1888

Lizzy Pierson Being duly sworn says:

I know Defendant Pierson; I am his wife. I know Dixon. Dixon is my husband's brother-in-law. We were eating breakfast on a Sunday morning. Smith's wife stepped outside of the tent to the fire and said "Dave, yonder comes the Marshal's with Winchesters." By the time she said this Dave had the baby and she grabbed the baby out of his arms. About this time one of the Marshal's poked his gun in the tent and Dave went and got his gun and Dave's wife and grabbed hold of the muzzle of the Marshal's gun and pushed the Marshal back. And Dave got his gun and they commenced shooting. They all shot at once, Dave was shooting at the marshals, I could not tell who shot first as I was under the tent when they shot while Dave Smith fell. Towerly was in the tent and he stayed in. Me and my husband got out with my baby. I had the baby when we came back, 2 were dead and 2 were wounded. Dixon's wife was dead and the Marshal was dead. We were eating breakfast when the marshals came up. Dave got out of the edge of the tent when he got his gun. His gun was sitting against the wall of the tent, back on the tent a piece. When he got his gun he went to the front of the tent and raised his gun, when he did so there were 2 or 3 shots fired and he fell. I think he and the Marshal fired at about the same time. I could not see I was back under the tent sitting by the table, me and my husband never got up until Dave Smith fell. When Dave fell he, Dixon, ran out. He had not arms and he took hold of Dave. Dixon's wife was following him. Just as my husband and I started out of the tent I seen Mrs. Dixon holding Dixon. She had hold of his arm. They were down holding Dave and she shouted that Dave was killed. That is the last I seen and me and my husband run off. I did not see Dixon when he fell nor when he was shot, I do not know when he was shot. When we left, my husband and I, he was before me and he had hold of my arm. We went in the direction of the house where Mr. Roft's folks lived and we meet a woman and a man coming. We meet Mrs. Roft and Mr. Johnson. After the shooting Johnson and my husband went up to the tent. We waited there until the shooting was over. There was just a pistol and a gun in the tent. The gun belonged to Smith and the pistol to Towerly. When we got out we left Towerly in the tent with his pistol in his hands trying to get right and dodging from one crack to another. The Marshal that poked his gun in the tent did not fire in the tent, there were no shots fired in the tent. I do not think Towerly fired any before he went out. I do not know what Mr. Dixon and Mrs. Dixon were doing when he, Dixon, was shot. I could not tell much about it. I was scared and was for getting away. Mr. and Mrs. Dixon were sitting at the end on the table next to the door of the tent and we were at the far end back of the tent. Mr. and Mrs. Dixon went out before we did. When we got away from there Dixon nor his wife had not been hurt or shot.

Wherefrom Deft Pierson is discharged.

J. K. Pierson duly sworn in says:

We were all sitting in the tent eating breakfast and Mrs. Smith, she got up from the table and stepped out to the front of the tent to get some bread. And she said to her husband, who was sitting at the table with his child in his arms "Dave here's a man with a Winchester" and he said "Take this child" she took the child and he made a jump for his gun. As he made the jump a man stuck a muzzle of a gun in the tent. I cannot say who it was she jumped at the man and hollered but I do not know what she said. She caught holt of the gun and shoved the gun back and by this time Smith was on his feet and had his gun. Smith jumped out of the tent. Just as he jumped out with his gun in his hands there were about 3 shots fired. There was hardly any distinction between them. Just about the time the 3 shots were fired me and my wife came out of the tent. Towerly came out a little behind us and ran around the tent like this is all I seen until I came back to the tent after the difficulty. Dixon and his wife were sitting at the table and raised up about the same time we did and they were going out of the tent just a little before us. They ran to Smith and both took hold of him and Mrs. Dixon hollered that he was killed. This is all I seen until I came back to the tent. Mr. Dixon nor Mrs. Dixon were not wounded or hurt the last I seen of them. I do not know what they were doing when they were shot. I never seen Mr. Cole there at all. I never seen Dalton until I came back to the tent after the shooting. I do not know where Mr. and Mrs. Dixon were shot. I never seen it. To the best of my knowledge, Smith fired first. I seen Towerly shoot one shot just as I came out of the tent. He was out at the front of the tent when he fired. Towerly came out a little piece behind me and fired when he came out. Mr. Dalton was said to be there in the direction he fired. There was not a shot fired from the inside of the tent while I was there. My wife and I ran some 60 yards from the tent. I met Mr. Johnson and Mrs. Roots. Mr. Johnson and I after the shooting went to the tent and we found Mr. Dalton and Mrs. Dixon dead and Mr. Dixon and Smith wounded. As I turned around to go to the tent after the shooting I seen Towerly leave the tent with a Winchester, bridle and saddle blanket in his hands. The only arms in the tent were a Winchester belonging to Smith and pistol belonging to

Smith. Towerly had his pistol. I did not see Dixon have any arms or with any arms.

It is appearing from the foregoing evidence to the satisfaction of the Commissioner that the offense with which the said Leander Dixon is charged, has been committed, and that there is probably cause to believe him guilty thereof, it is ordered that he stand committed.

James Brizzolara,
United States Commissioner for the Western District of Arkansas

I James Brizzolara do hereby certify that the foregoing is a true manuscript of the evidence taken before me, and the proceedings had in the above intitled cause and that the cost in said case are as follows:

Commissioners' fees $27.65
Witnesses' fees $34.45
Attendance of US Attorney

Frank Dalton's Testimony

Before me, Thos. B. Hardin Jr., Examiner Department of Justice, personally appeared one Frank Dalton, who upon being by me first duly sworn according to law, deposes and says:

I reside in Fort Smith, Arkansas, and am a Deputy U.S. Marshal, having received my first commission about the 7th of March 1886, and that commission having expired and been renewed on September 7, 1886.

I remember the circumstances of the arrest of William Washington. I had a writ for him issued by Commissioner Wheeler, charging the said Washington with "threatening to kill" and I arrested him near Coffeeville Kansas, about April 18, 1886, and took him to my camp near that place. Coffeeville Kansas is about two hundred and fifty miles from Fort Smith.

My next arrest after Washington on this trip was Dolly Hatfield. After arresting William Washington, we remaned in camp near Coffeeville about one week waiting for the arrival of some writs from Fort Smith. The writs did not come and at the end of the week we broke camp and started for Fort Smith with the prisoner Washington. We came on through Muscogee, not stopping there, and after traveling about ten days from Coffeeville we reached Childers Station in the Indian Territory. It did not take us ten days to travel two hundred and twenty miles, but part of the ten days was taken up by stoppage while I was endeavoring to arrest other persons for whom I had writs. I had writs for among other, one Lattimore Sanglobki and William Pidgeon, but I arrested none of these names.

At Childers Station I arrested Dolly Hatfield for whom I also had a writ. The night of her arrest, I left my posse at her home to guard her and I went to my camp about one mile away. The next morning my posse brought her into camp and we again started for Fort Smith, reaching there the same day Dolly Hatfield was arrested I think on May 6, 1886 and we reached Fort Smith on May 7.

On the same day that we arrived in Fort Smith, I placed William Washington in jail and a few minutes afterwards I was told by Commissioner Wheeler that Washington had already been tried and released on the charge for which I had arrested him, and he must be released. Accordingly, I discharged him from custody. The writ for Washington's arrest had been placed in my hands about one month before, and had never been called in, nor did I know of his having ever been tried on this charge. I do not remember whether or no Washington told me at the time of his arrest that he had been tried and released, but if he did, I did not believe him as I knew he had been "on the scout". He had not been arrested on this charge, as I afterwards learned, but had come to Fort Smith and given himself up.

On the night of our arrival in Fort Smith with Washington and Dolly Hatfield in custody, Dolly Hatfield secured an attorney who agreed to be responsible for her appearance before the Commissioner on the next day, and pursuant to this agreement she was released by order of either Marshal Carroll or Commissioner Wheeler, or both- I do not now remember which. I cannot say whether the lawyer gave bond for Hatfield or whether she was released informally. The next day however Dolly Hatfield appeared before the Commissioner Wheeler and after a hearing she was bound over to court, gave bond and was released. This was on May 8.

These (Dolly Hatfield and William Washington) were the only two arrests made by me on this trip. Jesse Campbell was my posse on this trip, and Bob Dalton was employed as guard.

On my next trip, I left Fort Smith about May 18, 1886, ferrying the Arkansas River at that place, and charging the ferryage in my account as 'expenses endeavoring to arrest'. On May 20th or about two days later, I reached Webbers Falls, and ferrying the Arkansas river then, charged the same in my account also as above. Two days later, or about May 22, I again ferried the Arkansas River near Muscogee Indian Territory and charged the ferryage again as "expenses endeavoring to arrest". About five days later, or on or about May 27th I made my first arrest, by arresting Thomas B. Madden about four or five miles south of Coffeeville. For the subsistence of myself, posse, and guard, during the time while I started from Fort Smith, and May was 27th, the date on which my first arrest was made, I charged in my account as "expenses endeavoring to arrest" and at the rate of fifty cents each per day. The additional item for the subsistence of self and posse five days at fifty cents each per day, I do not remember how it was incurred. Beside the above I also charged as "expenses while endeavoring to arrest" for the subsistence of five head of horses for fifteen days.

After my arrest of Madden on May 27, he was taken to my camp near Coffeeville. From when he was arrested to Muscogee is, about one hundred miles. I next arrested Mose Green about two days after Madden was arrested and about twenty miles southwest of Coffeeville.

I took him also to my camp near Coffeeville. I next arrested Charles Chambers; I think the next day after Green was arrested. I arrested him about ten or fifteen miles south of Coffeeville and took him also to my camp near that place. The day after Chamber's arrest or about May 31st I arrested John and Ben Long. I arrested them about twenty miles southeast of Coffeeville and took them to my camp near that place. I arrested John Kerr, Chas. Kerr and Lewis Ross about two days after the arrest of John and Ben Long or about June 2nd. I arrested them about twenty miles from Coffeeville and between twenty-five and thirty miles from where the Longs were taken and they too were taken to my camp near Coffeeville. Almost immediately after the arrest of the Kerr brothers and Ross I moved my camp from near Coffeeville down to within five miles of Bartlesville Cherokee Nation, Indian territory June 6, 1886. I arrested John Kerr and E.B. Kerr on a charge of murder. I arrested them at or near Bartlesville and took them to my camp. We then broke camp and went to Muscogee when I arrested Thomas Gwinn on a charge of larceny and carried him to my camp. The next day after my arrival at Muscogee and some six or seven days after the arrest of the Kerrs, I took them, John and E. B. Kerr before Commissioner Tufts and after a hearing he bound them over to court. The next day I took the Long boys–John and Ben Long before him and he bound them over to court. I next carried before him the two Kerr boys and Lewis Ross who were also bound over and gave bond. Thomas Madden and Thomas Gwinn also had hearing here and were bound over.

We remained at Muscogee about four days and then started for Fort Smith reaching the latter place in about three days more. I brought with me to Fort Smith the prisoners named above as having been bound over by Commissioner Tufts—Thomas Madden, John and Ben Long, E.B. Kerr, and John Kerr and Thomas Gwinn. I also brought with me Mose Green who was not tried before Commissioner Tufts because the writ in his case was made returnable before Commissioner Wheeler at Fort Smith. On my arrival there he was tried before Commissioner Wheeler and being unable to give bond was placed in jail–having been held by the said Commissioner. Charles Chambers I also brought with me to Fort Smith and then placed him in jail, the writ in his case had been issued under an indictment by the grand jury.

Henry White had been arrested by Deputy Marshal William Fields, had been tried before Commissioner Tufts at Muscogee and by said Commissioner bound over and he was turned over to me by Deputy Fields. I carried him to Fort Smith and placed him in jail.

On my next trip I left Fort Smith about July 25th and proceeded to Coffeeville and from then to Old Parker Kansas, near which place I located my camp. I then arrested in the Indian Territory, but near Old Parker, one James Flatrock on a charge of larceny. E.B. Harrison, U.S. Commissioner at Fayetteville has issued the writ, out at the time of the arrest it was in the hands of another Deputy. The writ was never in my possession but when I returned with the prisoner to Fort Smith, the information on which it was issued was furnished me on which to make out my account. After Flatrock was arrested I took him to my camp near Old Parker. I arrested him on or about August of 1886. It is two hundred and fifty miles from where I arrested James Flatrock to Fort Smith. I had Flatrock in my custody before delivering him to the jailor at Fort Smith about three weeks. Two days afterward or about August 6th, I arrested Joe Bryan and took him to my camp near Old Parker. From said camp near Old Parker to where Bryan was arrested it is about one hundred miles, and from Fort Smith to the place of his arrest it is about three hundred miles. I had Joe Bryan in my possession and fed him for about three weeks. We then moved our camp down to and located it about one half mile from Vinita, Indian Territory. From here I rode out with my posse and arrested Bruce Miller and John Wallace. We arrested Miller and Wallace about forty miles from Okmulgee, Creek Nation and about seventy-five miles from the place of Joe Bryant's arrest. We took Wallace and Miller to our camp near Vinita. Miller was arrested about a week after Joe Bryant was arrested, and John Wallace was arrested on the next day after Miller. I had Miller and Wallace in my custody about twelve days. I had about twenty miles extra riding to subpoena the witnesses against Miller and Wallace. I next arrested Richard Fields, at Vinta, Indian Territory, and about one week after the arrest of Wallace. Fields was taken to our camp near Vinita. We next arrested one Dirt Thrower, about twenty-five miles East of Vinita and took him to our camp. It is about sixty-five miles from where Dirt Thrower was arrested to Muscogee, and I arrested him on the next day after I arrested Fields.

The next man arrested was Ike Little Dove. I arrested him near Manns Mills, Cherokee Nation, and about forty miles southeast of Vinita. It is about twenty miles from where Dirt Thrower was arrested. I think I arrested Little Dove the next day after Dirt Thrower was arrested, but I cannot state positively. I took Little Dove to our camp near Vinita.

We then moved our camp down to Muscogee, it taking about three days to reach that place with our wagon. At Muscogee I arrested Black Hoyt on a charge of personating a U.S. officer. I took Black Hoyt before Commissioner Tufts at Muscogee immediately after his arrest, and after a hearing he was held for court, gave bond and was released. I also on the same day we reached Muscogee–at least I think it was the same day, took Bruce Miller and John Wallace before Commissioner Tufts. After a hearing they were held for trial, gave bond and were released. Either the same day or the next, I do not now remember which, I took Richard Fields before Commissioner Tufts, who held him for court, when Fields gave bond and was released. I also took Dirt Thrower before the said Commissioner who held him for trial, and as he was unable to give bond he was remanded to my custody. This left in my custody James Flatrock, Joe Bryan, Dirt Thrower and Ike Little Dove.

Of these named prisoners, I carried them all to Fort Smith, it taking about three days to go from Muscogee to Fort Smith. At Fort Smith I took Flatrock, Bryan, and Little Dove before U.S. Commissioner Wheeler, and committed Dirt Thrower to jail. This was done the same day I got to Fort Smith I think, though it is possible the trials of the first three men did not take place before the Commissioner until the next day. I took Bryan and Little Dove before Wheeler and not before Tufts because the writs for them had been issued by the first named Commissioner, and I took Flatrock before him because I thought the writ for the said Flatrock had been issued by Commissioner Wheeler, thought I afterwards learned it had been issued by Commissioner Harrison of Fayetteville. As I have before stated, this last-named writ was not in my possession.

Flatrock waived examination after the Commissioner and he was committed to jail. Bryan was discharged, the Commissioner declining to hold him. Little Dove was held for trial and in default of bond was committed to jail. Jesse Campbell was my posse on this trip, and Bill Collins and Bob Dalton were my guards.

My next and last trip was begun on November 6, 1886. I left Fort Smith on that date and went to Gibson Station Indian Territory. There or near there I arrested Richard Sutherland on a charge of murder, the writ being issued under an indictment found against him, I arrested him on November 8th, and brought him to Fort Smith, reaching the last-named place on November 11th. I committed him to jail at Fort Smith. It is about one hundred miles from where I arrested Sutherland to Fort Smith. I only arrested this one man on this trip. Bud Heady was my posse and I had no guard.

I have presented no account against the Government for the arrest of any other person or persons besides those I have named in this affidavit. Is my custom to register my posse as required by the Marshal and my guard I pay the same mileage as is allowed to me for his service. And in my account, I charge for the services of a guard from the time I arrest the man being furthest from Fort Smith.

I make my charge in my account for the subsistence of prisoners vary according to the price paid for the provision I buy. I generally charge though from sixty to seventy cents per day for each prisoner. I do this because I have calculated that this is about a just price.

I now remember that I did not get the writ for Dolly Hatfield until after I got back to Fort Smith from the trip on which she was arrested.

Frank Dalton

Sworn to before me and subscribed in my presence this 13th day of November. A.D. 1886, at Fort Smith Arkansas.

Thos. B. Hardin Jr.
Examiner Dept of Justice

HOUSTON PAYNE

My full name is Houston J. Payne. The first I remember noticing of Spencer after the boat landed he was holding up a bottle of whiskey and saying "Yes I have got whiskey" and he made the remark "Yes I have got whiskey and you can get it." I don't know what reply MR Cole made. I was some distance off and there was right smart racket; he was shaking it in his hand and the whiskey, the best I remember it was on his right side; I couldn't see whether it was in his left or right hand. It seemed to me that the whiskey was on the right side. Just about the time he said that he throwed his pistol down. I thought it was in an elevated position. I thought it went over Mr. Cole. As he threw his pistol down he fired and it wasn't just an instant until I saw Mr. Cole's arm move and just as his arm got level he fired and this man fell. As soon as he fell the crowd began to gather around there and I couldn't hardly tell what went on after that. Several was getting away from there pretty fast and several was fathering around the body. He died in a few minutes; I never heard him say a word. I don't think he gasped more than twice after I went to him, I suppose it was a minute after I went to him. I was on my horse all the time and Mr. Cole motioned to me to come to him and I got off my horse and went to him. I don't think he gasped more than twice after I went to him; I couldn't say positive which hand his pistol was in but to the best of my knowledge it was in his right hand and his whiskey in his left holding it sorter over to the right side. His pistol fell out of his hand after he fell, and I think Mr. Harris picked it up; I don't think Spencer was drinking. On the boat, he come up and spoke to Simpson on the boat and pulled a paper out of his pocket and went off and commenced reading. He wasn't disorderly on account of whiskey I don't think. I don't think he was drinking.

About the Author

Harold Trisler

I waited until I was seventy to write my first book. Maturity was always a trait that I admired in authors. I finally decided to give up on achieving maturity and just go ahead and write the book.

My academic literary education culminated in 1970 when I successfully completed freshman English on the first try. I do a little better on the history side.

I know a lot of living historians. I am a reenactor. I will tackle alongside of my talented wife anything from the war of 1812 to late 1800s trials of Judge Isaac Parker. I engage from the

1999 Booshway of the SWRR, a Civil War Artilleryman, to the Sheriff and regional Vice President of Westerners International.

I supported my hobby by being a registered nurse for some forty odd years. I was the head of an inpatient psychiatric unit for twenty-five years. The Fort Smith hospital where I worked had as its first chairman of the board Judge Parker. It is all history.

I have been involved in several historical films, including the *Trial of Bass Reeves*, which was the first fund raiser for the Bass Reeves statue project. I have now started writing my second book—still no maturity in sight.

About the Contributor & Editor

David Higginbotham

David Higginbotham is a writer and editor from Fort Smith, Arkansas. David is a former backcountry guide in the Sangre de Cristo Mountains and Boundary Waters Canoe Area who was a college professor for twenty years before leaving academia for a career in marketing.

Acknowledgements

This is where I acknowledge that— boy did I need a lot of help! A lot of this is already in the book but this is the formal thank you note. Thanks, ya'll. I need to start with Dave Higginbotham, that is where the book started. He literally molded my mess into a book. He is my contributor, editor, shepherd, guide, and saint. No Dave–no book.

You may be surprised to learn that I am still married. Dave was great, but he did not have to live with me. My wife and love of fifty years now, suffered right along with me though every agonizing word. She always had faith that somewhere in there was something that made sense. Her passion for this subject carried us through every time. No Suz–no Harold.

Thanks to Al Drap for encouraging this quest from the start. Roy Schirmer helped in many ways. His greatest contribution was telling me about the Pebley Center at the University of Arkansas–Fort Smith (UAFS). Shelley [Two e's, please] Blanton, the Pebley Center Archivist, was amazing. She did all the computer research for this book. My idea of the Payne–Moffett connection was confirmed by her research.

Cody Faber and Loren McLane from the Fort Smith National Historic Site supported my fumbling through history with patience and much needed editing. Their support validated the whole project.

Tom Wing, Assistant Professor UAFS, legitimized my ideas from the start. I will never forget sitting with him at the Drennen House in Van Buren, which he directs, and having him acknowledge my work to the point of recommending me to his publisher.

Dave Turk, the official Historian for the whole dang U.S. Marshal Service, endorsed my project! He even wanted to see the house from the book. He also kindly gave us notes on the book.

Profound heartfelt thanks to all.